The Step-by-Step Guide to

PATIO AND CONTAINER
GARDENING

COURAGE
BOOKS

AN IMPRINT OF RUNNING PRESS
PHILADELPHIA • LONDON

© 1997 CLB International, Godalming, Surrey, UK

First published in the United States in 1997 by Courage Books

Printed in Hong Kong by Sing Cheong

9 8 7 6 5 4 3 2 1
Digit on the right indicates the number of this printing

Library of Congress Cataloging-in-Publication Number 96-86626

ISBN 0-7624-0122-2

Compiled and edited: Ideas Into Print
Design layouts: Jill Coote
Step-by-step photographs: Neil Sutherland
Production Director: Gerald Hughes
Production: Ruth Arthur, Neil Randles, Karen Staff

Picture Credits
The majority of the photographs featured in this book have been taken by Neil Sutherland
and are © CLB International. The publishers wish to thank Eric Crichton and John Glover for providing additional
photographs.

This book may be ordered by mail from the publisher. *But try your bookstore first!*

Published by Courage Books
an imprint of Running Press Book Publishers
125 South Twenty-second Street
Philadelphia, Pennsylvania 19103-4399

Contents

Introduction

A patio is often described as an outdoor room, but it is actually halfway between the house and the garden, containing elements of both. From indoors, there are the furniture, floor coverings and potted plants; while from outdoors there is the weather, which means that you need to use plants, surfacing and "hardware" durable enough to withstand the climate. A patio provides a unique gardening environment that makes it possible to grow many kinds of slightly tender or delicate plants, usually sunlovers, that may prove difficult or unsatisfactory when grown in the open garden. There is also the opportunity to make full use of plants in containers and beds or on walls to soften the hard lines of the patio and the house. So, whether you use plants to decorate the patio or the patio to house your favorite plants, you will be spoilt for choice!

SITING THE PATIO

The patio is essentially an outdoor living area, a firm, dry level surface where you can relax in the sunshine or enjoy an alfresco meal. Although the most convenient place for a patio is close to the house, try and site it where it will receive maximum sunshine. This may mean a spot at the opposite end of the garden, in which case provide some form of permanent dry access from the house, such as a path or stepping stones. The size and shape of your patio can be an important element in the overall impact and success of your garden. If the traditional square or rectangle looks too formal or does little for a small, regular plot, experiment with curves and circles. Break up areas of hard landscaping with a change of level or integrated features, such as raised beds, a patio pool, built-in furniture or even a barbecue. Sometimes the choice of paving materials will influence the final shape and size of the area, so it makes sense to have some idea of how you want the patio to look before you make your final decision. If you can calculate the area using complete bricks, blocks or pavers, you will save yourself a lot of cutting and fitting at the construction stage, as well as expensive waste of materials.

Patios in the sun

Observe your garden to establish which areas are the sunniest at certain times. Put in two or even more patio areas, each designed to catch the sun at different times of the day.

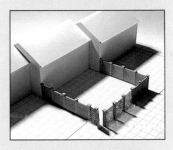

Above: Here, the house shades the area just beyond the back door for most of the day.

Above: Sometimes it is better to site the patio at the further end of the garden, if this is where it will receive the most sunshine.

Right: *In the garden design shown here, the main patio is situated immediately behind the house, as this is the area that receives maximum sunshine right through the day.*

Introducing a curve and a slight change of level is instantly softer and changes the whole look of the garden. Use your imagination at the early planning stages.

A free-standing patio makes an interesting option providing it can be well sheltered. Here, a circle is a good choice to liven up a regular square plot.

SLABS ON SAND WITH DRY MORTAR

Fixed paving slabs are not always necessary or desirable. If you want to alter the patio layout at a later date, it will be easier if you only have to lift the slabs. Such slabs can simply rest in place while those around them are mortared down permanently. If you use very large, heavy slabs, cement may not be necessary at all, especially if the patio surface will not take much weight. Even if they are not cemented down, you can still fill the cracks between the slabs with mortar to stop weeds growing. Later, you can remove the slabs with a crowbar after chipping the mortar loose; clean the edges before reusing the slabs. Alternatively, leave the cracks between slabs open, perhaps filled with gravel, and sow rock plants between them. Prepare the site by excavating a few inches of soil and consolidate the ground using crushed rubble or ballast covered by building sand, raked firm and leveled. Leave a 6in gap between the dampproof course and the planned upper surface of the patio, and allow a very slight slope away from the house to deflect water during heavy rain.

3 This method is easy to do and leaves the slabs clean; the alternative - pushing wet mortar down between the cracks - takes ages and makes a terrible mess.

1 Lay the slabs a finger's width apart - you can tap in wooden pegs as temporary spacers. Brush dry mortar into the cracks.

2 Water the slabs briskly with a fine rose. This washes the mortar in, wets it enough so that it can set and cleans the slabs.

Below: *Vary the pattern of the slabs by letting in an occasional block of bricks or planting pocket, here featuring lilies and*

Containers act as focal points to break up the horizontal symmetry of a patio.

Keep everything dry at this stage so that the mortar runs into the cracks.

BEDS IN PAVING

One way of livening up a large area of paving is to make sunken beds by removing occasional slabs and planting in the spaces. If you are laying a new patio, simply leave the soil clear where the bed is to go. Improve the existing garden soil (assuming it is reasonably good) with organic matter, such as well-rotted garden compost, and pave round it. If you want to take up slabs from an existing paved area, chip away the cement from between the slabs and lever them out with a crowbar. If they are completely bedded into cement, you may not be able to avoid cracking them, and you may need a power hammer to remove them, together with the foundations beneath, until you reach bare soil. Once the slabs are out, excavate as much rubble as you can and then refill with good topsoil, enriched with some extra organic matter. You could leave the bed 'flush' with the paving, or make a low raised edge to it using bricks or rope-edged tiles.

Plants for paving

Because the surrounding slabs keep roots cool and prevent evaporation, the soil dries out much more slowly than potting mixture in containers. The plants have a bigger root run, too. The following plants will flourish in paving: *Acaena, Alchemilla mollis, Cistus, Dianthus, Diascia,* ericas, *Frankenia, Helianthemum,* junipers, rosemary, sedums, *Sisyrinchium,* thymes & sages.

4 Planting compact rock plants in the corners 'ties in' the bed with rock plants growing in the cracks between other slabs nearby.

Potentilla fruticosa 'Red Robin'

Saxifraga 'Beechwood White'

Sedum 'Lydium'

Tuck some gravel around and under the plants for decoration and drainage.

Festuca glacialis

1 Lift out the slab - this one is easy as it is only loose-laid over soil. Excavate the hole so that there is room to put in plenty of good soil to sustain the plants.

2 If the existing soil is reasonably good, simply add some suitable organic matter to improve the texture and help moisture retention.

3 Put the largest plant in the center of the new bed. This potentilla is compact and bushy, with a long flowering season throughout the summer.

5 Plant all four corners for a neat look. Choose plants that contrast in color and shape, and that will spill out over the surrounding paving as they grow.

CRAZY PAVING

Crazy paving aptly describes the effect created when pieces of randomly shaped stone are interlocked to create a hard surface. It is economical to buy, making use as it does of broken pieces of square or rectangular paving that would otherwise go to waste. The stones fit together like the pieces of a jigsaw and the gaps between them are pointed with mortar, which bonds the stones to a stable subbase. An old concrete surface would make an ideal subbase for a driveway or parking place, but well-rammed coarse aggregate is suitable for light-duty areas, such as patios or paths. Crazy paving can look very attractive if you fit the pieces together carefully and neatly detail the pointing. Try mixing stones of different hues and textures or use mortar pigments in the pointing that contrast with the colors of the stones.

3 Set the corner stone in place, tamp it down into the mortar bed using a wood offcut to protect the surface against damage and check the levels in both directions.

4 Complete one edge of the area, including the next corner stone. Build up the jigsaw effect with large and smaller stones.

Position the next corner stone, tamp it down and check that it is level with its neighbor.

Allow a slope of 1 in 40 away from adjacent buildings or across freestanding paths and drives.

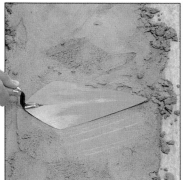

1 A solid concrete or well-rammed aggregate subbase is essential. Spread a bed of fairly sloppy mortar along the perimeter of the subbase.

2 Choose relatively large stones with two adjacent straight edges to form the corners of square or rectangular paved areas.

5 As you extend the area of paving, use a spirit level and a long wooden straightedge to check that the stones are level (or have a constant fall).

6 Allow the mortar bed to harden overnight, then fill and point the joints. Draw the trowel along the joint to leave a center ridge and two sloping levels.

LAYING BRICKS ON SAND

Laying bricks involves much the same technique as used for slabs. Prepare the base of rubble topped with building sand in exactly the same way. You can secure the bricks with blobs of mortar; two blobs of mortar are enough underneath each brick, one at each end. However, since bricks are smaller and thicker and less likely to slide about or rock than slabs, they can be laid loose and directly onto the sand. This is a good idea if you want to move them later – perhaps to open up beds or alter the shape of the paved area. It is also rather quicker to make a hard surface in this way than when using mortar, but the result is not quite as durable. Bricks laid straight into sand are most suitable for surfacing a paved area that will not get much heavy traffic over it. Since the bricks are not held in place with mortar, check them periodically and resit any that seem to have sunk or become uneven. This is most likely to happen in high rainfall areas or where heavy wheelbarrows, etc., are frequently pushed over the area and the weight bears unevenly over the bricks. However, used as intended, it is a perfectly good surface.

This kiln-dried joint filling sand is very fine, and trickles through the smallest gaps.

The pattern shown here is herringbone, one of the most popular and easy to lay.

Use both hands to lift bricks straight into place. Sit them squarely onto the sand; do not drop one end or it makes a depression that will make the finish uneven.

3 Decide on a pattern in which to lay the bricks; these are laid in alternate pairs. Practice laying bricks on a hard surface, away from the prepared base, to gain confidence.

Above: When the brickwork is completed and dry, tip a few buckets of dry sand onto it and smooth it into the cracks with a soft broom. The sand slides into the gaps easily.

1 Prepare the base layers of 2 inches of rubble and 1-2 inches of building sand, as described on page 6. Rake the sand level and firm it down lightly with the back of a

2 Check that the surface is level using a spirit level resting on a flat piece of wood, and smooth the surface over with this so that the sand becomes smooth and consistently firm.

4 Tap each brick lightly down at both ends with the handle of a hammer, so that it beds into the sand layer and ends up with the top completely flush with the bricks next to it.

LAYING COBBLES IN MORTAR

Cobblestones make a most attractive contrast to areas of flat paving. Use them in place of an occasional slab for a change of texture, to add decorative detail to larger areas or in an oriental-style garden. Rounded cobblestones are not very easy to walk on, so use them to guide people away from overhanging plants or to deter children from getting too close to a pond. When they are laid as decorative surfacing amongst plants, bed them loosely into the soil. This allows rainwater to run through and lets you change the design. However, if people are to walk on the cobbles, bed them into cement or mortar to hold them firmly in place. Since they can be slippery when wet, set cobbles so that about half of each stone is above the level of the cement base, leaving plenty of drainage space for water to run away between the stones. In a large area, lay cobbles on a very slight slope, the same as for paving slabs, so that water does not lie in puddles.

Be sure to check the level and tap down the stones before the mortar starts to set.

Left: A decorative inset made of pebbles within a larger area of paving. The stones are angled to produce the swirling pattern.

Weeds and moss

Dig out weeds with a narrow-bladed knife or eradicate them using a proprietary path weedkiller. This will kill any plant it touches, so take care to keep it off plants overhanging the paving or deliberately planted in it. Remove large weeds by hand first, as woody top growth persists even after it is dead. Where there is any open soil for plants, weeds can grow, too. Do not use path weedkillers round them as they will kill the plants as well. Weedkillers will not kill moss, nor is it a good idea to use proprietary mosskillers unless they specifically state that they can be used on paving - most do not. Dig out moss with an old knife or trowel instead.

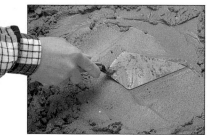

1 Make a boundary of wooden formwork around the working area and nail it roughly together. Pour in about 2 inches of rather wet mortar mix and smooth it out with a bricklaying trowel.

2 Choose even-sized cobbles, 2-3 inches in diameter, and press them about halfway down into the mortar. Stagger the rows slightly, so that adjacent cobblestones fit closely together.

3 Work a small area at a time and continue adding more stones until you have filled the area completely. Try to keep the surface of the cobbles as level as possible as you work.

4 Check the level by laying a piece of wood over the top. Gently tap any uneven cobbles into place with a hammer. Do not tap the cobbles directly, otherwise they may split.

LAYING A GRAVEL PATH

A path or other area of gravel can be an attractive feature in any garden, especially when used to provide a contrast alongside flat paving materials. True gravel is available in a range of mixed natural-earth shades that look particularly good when wet. You can also buy crushed stone in colors ranging from white through reds and greens to gray and black. Carefully work out how much material to order. Decorative aggregates are sold in small carry-home bags, commonly weighing from 55 to 110 pounds, and by volume in large canvas slings or in loose loads that are delivered to your home. You will need a bulk delivery for all but the smallest areas. A cubic yard of gravel weighs well over a ton, and will cover about 12 square yards to a depth of about 3 inches.

1 Excavate the area until you reach solid subsoil. Set out preservative-treated boards around the excavated areas and drive in stout corner pegs.

2 Secure the boards to the pegs with galvanized nails. Add further pegs at 3-foot intervals all round to prevent the boards from bowing outwards later on.

3 The best way of discouraging weeds in a gravel path is to put down a porous membrane, such as this strong woven plastic sheeting, over the subsoil.

Firm the subsoil and remove any sharp stones before laying the membrane.

Take the time to ensure that the surface is smooth and level.

4 To form a firm base, cover the membrane with a layer of crushed rock or fine hardcore. You need at least 2 inches of rock on firm subsoil, more if it is soft.

5 Compact the layer with a heavy garden roller. Fill in any hollows and roll again until you no longer leave footprints.

6 Without disturbing the compacted subbase, spread out the gravel or decorative stone. Fill the area up to the level of the perimeter boards.

PLANTING THROUGH GRAVEL

One way of having a garden that is quick and easy to look after, yet full of interest, is to create a gravel garden. Here, plants are grown in beds covered with a deep mulch of gravel, which suppresses weeds and helps retain moisture. Unlike a conventional organic mulch that slowly rots, gravel lasts forever. To make the mulch totally effective against weeds – even persistent perennial ones – the answer is to put the gravel over a layer of plastic (which needs to be perforated to allow the soil to 'breathe'), or over heavy-duty, woven plastic landscape fabric. The most suitable plants for growing through a permanent mulch are trees, shrubs, roses, conifers, perennial herbs and shrubby rock plants, as these all have a definite main stem around which you can tuck the plastic. Bulbs, herbaceous plants and annuals are not very suitable; if you want to incorporate them, set aside special areas where the plastic is excluded, leaving only gravel. Many rock plants and hardy annuals will seed themselves happily into a gravel-only mulch, and the result can look natural and pretty. Simply pull up any that appear where you do not want them. However, expect a few weeds to appear, too.

1 Turn back the corners of the plastic to uncover a square of soil. Hold back the plastic by piling gravel or stones onto the corners so that it does not get in the way as you work.

2 Scoop out soil to make a planting hole slightly larger than the size of the pot the plant is growing in. Place this carefully into a bucket, as weeds may grow in soil left above the plastic.

3 Carefully knock the plant out of its pot, so that you do not disturb the roots. Lift it into the prepared planting hole, with its best side facing forwards.

4 Fill the space around the rootball with some of the spare soil. Tuck the flaps of plastic back round the plant, making sure that you cover the

5 Make a separate hole for each plant in a group to avoid creating large areas of open soil in which weeds could get a hold.

6 Use low, sprawling plants around the edge of a group, with taller upright kinds to the center or back, to create an 'island' of plants in which each one shows up as an individual.

Juniperus communis 'Compressa'

Red hot poker (Kniphofia)

Hebe 'Sutherlandii'

Golden marjoram

Hypericum

Helianthemum 'Ben Fhada'

USING STONES AND GRAVEL AS A DECORATIVE FEATURE

Here, large rounded boulders and smaller cobbles are arranged together and drought-tolerant plants added to complement them. This scheme could add interest to a large area of gravel, such as a drive, but choose a spot where it does not interfere with pedestrians or parking. Or try it within a patio, in a square where four paving slabs have been left out. Insert the plants through the hard foundation of the surrounding area of paving or gravel. Alternatively, leave a patch of bare soil to develop as a feature when laying the patio. If you do this, cover the soil with anti-weed mulch fabric (see page 13), insert the plants through it and cover it with gravel. A feature like this has a definite 'front' to it and should face the direction from which it is most often seen. If it is to be seen from all round, design it so that the largest stones and tallest 'key' plants are in the middle, with smaller groups around them.

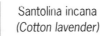

4 Spread a layer of fine gravel between the stones and plants. Rounded stones look best and are smoother than crushed gravel, which has sharp edges. Use just enough to cover the sand.

5 As the plants grow, they will partly obscure the stones and look quite natural. None will need pruning, although the cotton lavender can be trimmed lightly every spring or after flowering to keep it in shape.

The gravel acts as a 'mulch', helping to retain moisture around the plant roots. It will need 'topping up' every year or two, as some sinks into the sand below.

Juniper 'Blue Star'

Lamium 'Pink Pearls'

Acaena glauca (A low-growing New Zealand burr)

Santolina incana (Cotton lavender)

Viola labradorica

1 Arrange a group of large round stones on a base of rubble and building sand. Choose several similar stones, with one much larger and of a different color to make a contrast.

2 Lay a patch of cobbles – smaller, rounded stones, all the same color – onto the sand near the main group. Try adding a plant – here a juniper – to the group between the biggest stones.

3 Trowel out some of the sand and rubble to reach the soil beneath. Make a hole for each plant and add potting mixture. Remove the plants from their pots and put them in place.

WOODEN DECKING

Wooden decking is a natural alternative to hard paving in the garden. The raw material is widely available and much easier to cut to size than paving slabs or blocks. It is also more forgiving to walk on or sit down on than hard paving. The only disadvantages of wooden decking are that it will need occasional maintenance work and that it can be slippery in wet weather. Make sure that all the wood for the decking has been pretreated with preservative and apply a preservative stain to the entire completed structure. To keep the decking clear of damp ground and reduce the incidence of rot, set the joists on bricks, ideally with a pad of damp-course material or roofing felt between bricks and joists. Clear the ground beneath the decking with long-term weedkiller before you begin.

1 On firm ground, bricks are the simplest way of supporting the decking's joists. Space the joists evenly. Use a plank to align the joist ends and to check that their tops are level.

4 Leave a slight gap between the planks for drainage. Set a slim batten against the first plank and then position the second plank against the batten.

5 Secure the plank to each joist with two galvanized nails. If you wish, you can use a length of string as a guide to help you align the nail heads.

3 Cut the first decking plank to length, position it across the joists so its front edge projects over the fascia board and forms a projecting nosing. Secure it to each joist with two nails.

6 Wooden decking suits any garden and soon blends in with its surroundings as it weathers. You can link different levels with simple wooden steps.

There is no limit to the size and shape you can create.

2 Cut a fascia board to the width of the decking and nail it to the joist ends. Fix a batten across the joists at the other end of the decking.

Using containers

Choosing the most suitable container, preparing it for use and filling it with the right kind of potting mix are vital steps to success. This section provides the guidance you need.

Contents

CONTAINERS IN A SMALL GARDEN

In a small garden, containers are useful for turning otherwise unproductive space, such as paving, paths and steps – into colorful features. Stylish containers also help to establish the character of the garden, and it is worth buying matching sets of attractive, good-quality containers made of frostproof terracotta or painted and glazed ceramics. Although initially expensive, these will last for many years and look much better than cheap plastic containers. A wide range of planting schemes is possible. Annual bedding plants are the traditional choice, and provide maximum color during the summer. In the fall, you can put away the containers for the winter or replant them for a spring display. Alternatively, you can create a low-labor, all-year-round scheme using shrubby plants. Small trees could be trained flat and stood against patio walls where there is no soil bed. Since flowering shrubs tend to have short flowering seasons, it is best to create an all–year-round display using a mixture of flowering and foliage plants, including plenty of evergreen varieties.

Pieris forestii

Traditional oak barrel

Mediterranean style terracotta pot

Reconstituted stone octagonal tub

Textured pot made from reconstituted paper

Small terracotta pot cover with potted double primroses

Wooden trough

Oriental ceramic pot

Terracotta effect plastic pot

Classic-style square terracotta pot

HANGING BASKETS

You will find a huge range of hanging baskets in shops and garden centers, and most of them can be reused for many years simply by replacing the potting mixture and plants at the end of each season. The traditional wire–framed kind must be lined before use. Moss or a modern substitute, such as coco fiber, is the traditional choice. These look good and allow a wire basket to be planted up through the sides as well as the top, but they do not hold water very well, so the basket drips and needs frequent watering. Alternatively, try rigid liners made of reconstituted paper and flexible fabric, or 'whalehide'. You can make your own liner by cutting black plastic or capillary matting (sold for greenhouse benches) to shape. These do not look so good initially, but you can cut holes in the sides to plant through so they will soon be hidden by flowers and foliage – and they improve water retention.

Solid plastic baskets do not need lining and often incorporate their own water reservoir or drip tray, which saves them drying out so fast. If frequent watering is a problem, mix water–retaining gel crystals with the potting mix before planting up hanging baskets and wall planters, and line the inside of the container with absorbent fabric, such as capillary matting. Line porous containers with plastic. Automatic watering systems can be fitted up to take care of baskets on a regular basis.

Traditional wire basket with a liner made of reconstituted paper. Note the 'push-out' panels for planting through the sides.

Plastic self-watering hanging basket

Large terracotta wall pot. Being porous, terracotta pots dry out quickly.

Plastic self-watering wall planter

Terracotta wall planter

Natural sphagnum moss. This water-retentive material is traditionally used to line baskets. There are many modern alternatives.

Hanging pot with built-in drip tray

Coco fiber basket liner

Metal 'hayrack' wall planter (needs a liner)

Coco-moss (natural coco fiber dyed green)

CROCKING OPTIONS

Flowerpots come in two basic types: clay and plastic. Clay pots are porous, so the potting mixture in them dries out quickly due to evaporation through the sides. They are much heavier than plastics and the central drainage hole must be covered with a crock to prevent the soil washing away. Being lighter, plastic pots are the natural choice for roof gardens, hanging baskets and some windowboxes and wall pots. The potting mixture in them is slower to dry out as the sides of the pot are impervious to water, so take care when watering in dull conditions or when the plants are young or sickly and using less water than usual. Plastic pots are easier to clean and take up less storage space, as they fit inside one another.

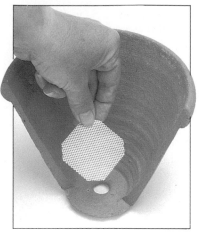

Above: Woodlice, earthworms and slugs can get into pots through the drainage holes. To prevent this, cover the holes with plastic or the fine metal mesh sold for vehicle bodywork repairs.

Above: A spring collection of tulips, narcissi, violas and yellow pansies are shown off to advantage in terracotta pots.

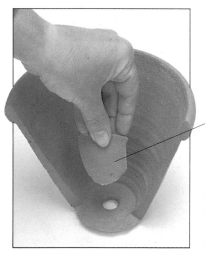

Clay pots have porous walls

Pieces from broken clay pots are known as 'crocks'.

Plastic pots have thin impervious walls.

Plastic pots usually have a ring of small drainage holes round the base.

Left: Place a large piece of broken clay flowerpot, curved side up, over the drainage hole. Recycle broken clay pots by smashing them with a hammer.

Above: Clay containers have large holes in the base that need covering with crocks. These keep the soil in, but allow the surplus water to drain out.

Above: Plastic pots, with their small holes, need no crocking, as soil is unlikely to escape through them, especially the coarser textured peaty potting mixtures.

LINER OPTIONS

Traditional wire hanging baskets must be lined before use. Moss-lined baskets look spectacular, as the wire framework allows you to plant the sides and base of the basket as well as the top, but they drip when watered and dry out quickly. Modern, solid-sided hanging baskets are easier to look after, but you cannot plant the sides. For the best of both worlds, use one of the modern liners inside a traditional basket.

Wire baskets must be lined before they will hold soil and plants; they are reusable for many years. Plastic-covered frames last longest.

Foam liners hold water well, can be cut to fit and are reusable. The overlapping flanges allow you to push plants through the sides of the basket. Choose natural colors.

Biodegradable, rigid liners are made of a compressed paperlike substance, colored and textured to resemble peat; they hold water well, but you cannot plant through the sides. They rarely last more than a year.

Black plastic liners that you cut to shape are disposable and hold water well, but are not very attractive. Cut holes to plant the sides of the basket and make sure that plants soon cover the container.

Reusable coco-fiber looks natural and can be cut to fit. The overlapping panels allow you to plant around the sides of the basket

Sphagnum moss in bags is sold especially for lining baskets. It looks very good, but needs a great deal of watering.

Flexible liners with fitted bases are designed for baskets with a particular base size, although you can trim them. Most kinds are reusable.

Left: You can buy a special hanging basket formula for baskets and wall pots. If you choose an ordinary mix, peat or coir are preferable, as they are lighter.

CHOOSING SOILS

Visit any garden center, and you will find a wide range of soils, grits, gravels, sands and chippings on sale. What to buy depends very much on what you plan to grow. The basic requirement is for a potting mixture. As a rule, a soil-based potting mixture is preferred for plants that are to be left in the same containers for more than one year, such as alpines and shrubs, because soil acts as a 'buffer' and holds more trace elements than peat products. A peat- or coir-based mixture is often preferred for annuals and other bedding plants or bulbs that only remain in the containers for one growing season. They tend to retain more water than soil-based mixtures, which dry out faster. Plants in a peat or peat-substitute mixture will need feeding after four to six weeks.

Below: Soil and peat-based mixes are the most common. An ericaceous mix is for lime-hating plants. Coir is a 'green' alternative to peat. Hanging basket mixes usually contain water-retaining ingredients.

Ericaceous mix

Hanging basket mix

Soil-based potting mixture

Peat-based, multipurpose mix

Coir-based mix

Left: Use a soil–based potting mixture for plants that are to stay in the same container for several years. Containers left outside in winter are more likely to remain upright in windy weather if filled with this heavier mixture.

CHOOSING SOILS

Below: *Horticultural, or potting, grit adds weight and air spaces to ordinary potting mixtures. It makes a good growing medium for plants that need particularly well-drained conditions.*

Right: *Grit, chippings and mulches improve drainage in potting mixes and decorate the surface of the soil.*

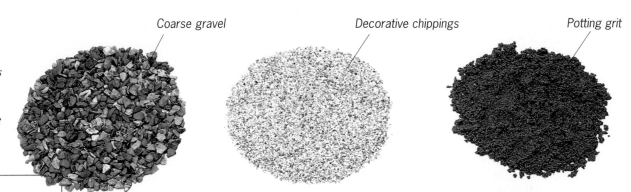

Coarse gravel

Decorative chippings

Potting grit

Cocoa shell

Bark chippings

Potting grit should contain a mixture of particle sizes, from fine sand to fine grit. Mix one part of grit to four of potting mixture.

Right: *Place a layer of coarse grit over the crocks in a trough for herbs or alpines, which need good drainage. Then add soil-based potting mixture for these plants and make sure it is not firmed down too hard, otherwise it will become waterlogged. Use grit in the base of pots with bulbs left outside through the winter; bulbs will rot if left in wet soil.*

WATERING AND FEEDING

The secret of successful containers lies in regular feeding and watering. To flower well over a long season, plants need a continuous supply of nutrients – if they go short, the flowering quickly suffers. If you forget to feed regularly, use slow-release fertilizer pills, granules or sachets. Check containers daily and water them whenever the potting mix feels dry. In a hot summer, well-filled containers in full bloom may need watering twice a day. If watering is a problem, there are various products and devices on the market to help you. Try self-watering pots or add a water retaining gel to the soil before planting. Terracotta 'water wells' have a wide neck with a spike-shaped base that you push into the soil. Water seeps slowly out through the porous sides so that the soil can absorb it gradually.

Slow-release fertilizer granules

You can mix slow-release fertilizer granules with the potting mixture before planting up a container. To 'top up' later in the season, simply sprinkle more granules over the soil or make a hole with a pencil and push the granules into it. Alternatively, you can buy small bags containing a measured dose of granules. Always read the manufacturer's instructions carefully to see how long you can expect slow-release feeds to last; individual products vary.

Above: Press slow-release fertilizer 'pills' firmly into the middle of the soil. Nutrients will slowly escape whenever the potting mix is moist.

Water-retaining gel

Mix the dry granules with water and stir to make a thick gel. Combine with the potting mixture. The gel crystals soak up surplus water for later release as the soil dries out.

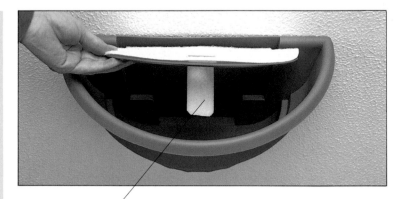

As the soil dries out, the wick draws up water.

Above: This wall basket has a water reservoir built into the base. It stores any surplus water that drains through from the soil above until it is needed.

MAKING A CONTAINER FROM HYPERTUFA

*G*enuine old stone containers, such as butlers' sinks, are highly sought after by collectors for growing alpines and are very expensive. But there is an alternative; you can now make your own containers from a fake stone mixture called hypertufa. The ingredients are available from any garden center or hardware store. It is cheap, and very versatile. You can cover an old ceramic sink, provided you first coat the shiny surface with outdoor-quality building adhesive. This gives it a rough surface to which the hypertufa can 'key in', otherwise the mixture just slides off. It is also possible to make your own 'stone' trough using the cardboard box method featured here.

Cement powder

*5*Mix equal parts by volume of cement, gritty sand and moss peat or a peat substitute. Add water to make a sloppy paste.

Peat or coir-based substitute

Coarse gritty sand

*1*Select two strong cardboard boxes that fit one inside the other, leaving a gap between them of 2 inches all round.

*2*Cut a piece of board to fit exactly inside the base of the larger, outer box. Nail four wine corks as shown these will eventually form the drainage holes in the base of the finished container.

*3*To reinforce the hypertufa, cut a piece of small-mesh chicken wire to cover the inner box entirely. Fold in the corners to form a loose cage very slightly bigger than the inner box.

*4*Slip the smaller box with its wire cover into the larger box. If the wire sticks out, bend it more firmly until it slips in easily.

6 *Remove the inner box and wire netting, and trowel enough hypertufa mixture over the board base to come to the top of the corks. Do not cover them.*

7 *Fit the inner box into the center so that the wire sinks into the hypertufa and there is an even gap between the boxes. Fill the gap with hypertufa.*

MAKING A CONTAINER FROM HYPERTUFA

Hypertufa can transform an old container, such as a clay flowerpot, into a stone one, just by giving it a new outer finish. If you have large terracotta pots that have cracked, a coating of hypertufa can hide a repair, where the broken pieces have been joined by a suitable adhesive. You could also cover a new pot. Start by soaking the flowerpot in water. This is particularly important if you are using a brand new pot. Then, wearing rubber gloves, press handfuls of the hypertufa all over the surface, remembering to coat the inside rim of the pot so that when it is planted the original surface is no longer visible. Stand the pot in a sheltered place to dry slowly and acquire a rough, stonelike texture. You can also make free-style containers from scratch, using the mixture to cover a foundation made of scrunched up small-mesh chicken wire.

10 *After six weeks, gently peel back the sides of the inner cardboard box to check if the hypertufa is 'done'. Even so, it will not be very firm, so treat it gently for several more weeks.*

8 *Use a piece of wood to ram the mixture down between the two boxes on each side of the wire so that there are no air pockets. These would turn out as holes in the sides of the finished container.*

Do not worry if the sides of the outer box bow out slightly; this will only improve the finished shape.

9 *Roughly round off and smooth the exposed surface of the hypertufa – this will form the edges of the container.*

THE CONTAINER EMERGES

Hypertufa takes a long time to dry out, so make the container where you will not need to move it or put it on top of a firm wooden base that you can lift without touching the sides of the container. Allow six weeks for a large sink or trough made by the cardboard box method to set before you remove the boxes. Do not worry if there are some imperfections, as they add character. Any air pockets left while the hypertufa was in the mold will be apparent as holes in the sides of the container. If they go right through, or can be enlarged to do so, transform them into side planting pockets. Hypertufa continues to dry after the mold is removed. When it is completely dry it turns a pale gray color, similar to stone. If you used coarse-textured sand and peat in the mix, it will also have a craggy texture. The longer you leave hypertufa containers in the open air, the more weathered they become. To speed up this process, spray the sides with diluted liquid houseplant feed. This encourages lichens and moss to colonize them, creating the look of a genuine aged stone container.

11 Remove the inner box by folding it inwards and then lifting out the base one end at a time. Take your time and work carefully, as forcing it may damage the container.

12 Cut away the cardboard from the sides of the container. Do not hurry or you may pull pieces of hypertufa away with the cardboard. Peel off loose paper shreds with your fingers.

A drop of liquid detergent in the water helps to remove scraps of cardboard.

Roughen up smooth surfaces with a wire brush.

13 Wet any slivers of paper left behind and peel them off with a knife or a wire brush. They will eventually disappear.

14 Turn the container over to remove the cardboard from the base. Prise the wooden board away from the base. The corks will be left behind in the hypertufa.

Drill through the corks to make the drainage holes.

15 The finished container is ready for planting. Raise it up on two bricks to allow surplus water to drain away.

PREPARING A GROWING BAG

In their simplest form, growing bags are just bags of potting mixture that you cut open and into which you can plant a wide range of both ornamental and edible plants. Growing bags have two main benefits. Firstly, the potting mixture they contain is completely free of the pests and diseases that often affect plants growing in the garden. The other is that they allow you to grow plants in all kinds of confined spaces, including yards, on balconies or windowsills and even on rooftops. There is still a certain amount of suspicion concerning growing bags and a feeling that they are something 'different'. They are not; they are simply another type of container specifically designed for growing plants in. The mixtures they contain are not general-purpose mixtures; they are formulated to produce the best results for the specific growing conditions. Growing bags can be used several times over, as long as you plant completely different crops each time. Plant cucumbers, tomatoes or peppers first, as these are the most sensitive to root problems, and follow with spinach, zucchini, potatoes and lettuce.

1 Make a V-shaped cut at one end and cut from the point of the V towards the center of the bag. (Most growing bags have printed guidelines that show you where to cut.)

2 Make two planting compartments by leaving a 'bridge' across the middle of the growing bag. This prevents the bag from spreading outwards too much when it is moved, being planted up or watered.

You may prefer simply to cut out the two squares, but folding the edges under makes a stronger job and creates raised sides that prevent water spilling out too easily.

Preparing a growing bag in position

If possible, prepare and plant up a growing bag in position. To prevent it spreading, surround it with, say, ornamental stones.

1 If you prefer, you can use a sharp knife to open a growing bag. Carefully even out the mixture in the bag.

2 Cut out a single planting compartment, as shown here. Do not spill the potting mix when refilling the corners.

1 Mix up a small amount of white, yellow and dark green artist's acrylic paint. Add water to make a fairly thin, runny mixture. Tilt the wallbasket back slightly and apply the first coat.

PAINT EFFECTS FOR WEATHERING PLASTIC

Plastic terracotta–effect pots tend to have a rather raw, brand new look. Over a period of time, real terracotta weathers and takes on the patina of age. White salt deposits work through to the surface and a coating of green algae often appears. Using a variety of simple paint techniques, it is possible to mimic this transformation and achieve a realistic effect on plastic containers. Pots and planters with a high relief are the most convincing when painted, as the dark and light shading emphasizes the contours. Artist's acrylic paint, mixed and thinned with water, is an ideal medium, as it remains wet and soluble for long enough to work on, but then dries to form an effective waterproof plastic coating.

6 Once the second coat has dried, mix up some dark green paint and water. Using a damp, natural sponge, work paint into all the crevices.

2 Cover the face with a liberal quantity of paint. You need not be too particular at this stage and you will notice that the color tends to run off the raised portions and collect in the grooves.

3 If the color is too opaque and the terracotta does not start to show through after a couple of minutes, use a clean, wet brush and go over the raised portions of the face again, diluting the paint.

4 Using a slightly damp pad of absorbent paper, dab patches of paint from the raised features. Once dry, apply a second coat. Adjust the color if necessary. Here, extra white and yellow were added.

5 The paint runs down in streaks, much like weathering caused by damp conditions. The pigments separate out, adding to the illusion of age.

TREATING A WOODEN BARREL BEFORE USE

Wooden half barrels are the favorite choice for permanently planting woodland shrubs, such as dwarf rhododendron, pieris or camellia, as they go so well together. You will need a large barrel, but do not choose one larger than you can comfortably move when it is full of soil. A 12-inch container is the very smallest you should consider; 15-18 inches is better and 24 inches the ultimate. The larger the container, the larger the plant will be able to grow, because there will be more room for the roots. In a small pot the plant will be naturally dwarfed, but it will also dry out very quickly and need more frequent watering. Bear in mind that lime-hating plants, such as rhododendron and pieris, must be planted in ericaceous soil. Many slow-growing or compact evergreen shrubs also make excellent specimen plants in a wooden barrel. Plant these in a good-quality peat- or soil-based potting mixture and feed and water well.

4 Take a square of unperforated plastic at least four times as wide as the barrel, lay it over the top and push the middle down to form a loose lining. Push the center 2 inches out through the hole in the base.

1 Drill a hole at least ½ inch in diameter in the base of the barrel. Alternatively, you could make a group of smaller holes.

2 A drainage hole is essential, especially for plants left outdoors in winter, otherwise the potting mix becomes waterlogged.

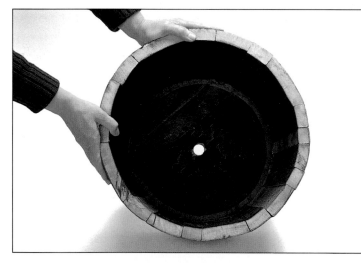

3 Paint the barrel inside and out, (not forgetting the base) with plant-friendly wood preservative. To allow paint fumes to disappear, leave the barrel to dry out for a few days before proceeding.

5 Cut the tip off the plastic sheet protruding through the hole in the base of the barrel. This allows the excess water to drain away from the potting soil without wetting the wood and thus reduces the risk of rotting.

Walls and trellis

Providing the right backdrop for your plant containers and attractive and functional support for climbers can transform your patio. This section sets out the options.

Contents

A STONE BLOCK WALL

Man-made garden walling blocks have flat tops and bottoms so that they can be laid and bonded easily, just like bricks. They are easier to cut than natural stone, using ordinary masonry tools, and readily available. The blocks are available in colors ranging from shades of gray to reds, buffs and yellows. Block sizes vary, but the commonest measures about 9 inches long, 4 inches wide and 2⅝ inches high. Some ranges include longer and thicker blocks, allowing you to build walls with irregular coursing as if using natural stone. You can leave the top course of the wall exposed, but it will look more attractive if you finish it with a row of matching coping stones, which are designed to help rainwater to run off and fall clear of the wall face below.

Use a mortar mix of 1 part cement, 1 part lime and 5 parts building sand.

3 After laying two or three whole blocks, use a spirit level to check that they are horizontal both along the wall direction and at right angles to it.

Neaten the vertical joints between the blocks. Spread a mortar bed on top for the second course.

4 Butter some mortar onto the end of each block before butting it up against its predecessor to leave a vertical joint about ⅜ inch thick.

1 Lay a concrete foundation 6 inches thick and twice as wide as the wall thickness. Bed the first course on a mortar bed along the building

2 To maintain the bonding pattern in the second course, place a half-block at one end of the wall. Cut it with a bricklayer's chisel and light sledge hammer.

5 When the wall is high enough, spread mortar on top of the final course of blocks and lay the coping stones in place.

6 Trim off excess mortar from all the joints and neaten them with the tip of your pointing trowel. Alternatively, recess them using an offcut of garden hose.

BUILDING A SCREEN WALL

By their very nature, brick and stone walls provide a solid structure that is ideal for boundary walls. However, there may be situations where you would prefer an open screen, perhaps to surround a patio without cutting out too much sunlight or to conceal an eyesore. Pierced screen walling blocks are one option. These square blocks are easy to build up into a see-through screen that you can either leave to weather naturally or decorate with masonry paint. The blocks are a standard 11⅜ inches square, so they build up into a regular 11¾ inch grid with a ⅜ inch thick mortar joint and are usually 3⅝ inches thick. Since they cannot be cut down in size any wall you build must be an exact multiple of 11¾ inches in length and height. You can use the blocks on their own to create a complete screen, building up end, corner and intermediate piers with specially shaped pilaster blocks that are sized so that three match the height of two walling blocks.

1 Spread a bed of mortar along the building line on your foundation strip and draw the tip of your trowel along it to create a series of ridges.

2 To build a free-standing wall, set the first pilaster block in place on the mortar bed. The end pier block shown here has one recessed face.

3 Set a spirit level on top of the block to check that it is level in both directions. If necessary, tamp it down with the handle of a hammer.

Fill the central cavity with a fairly dry mortar and ram it down.

6 Add the third pilaster block to build the end pier up to 24 inches. Add the second course of blocks. Trim excess mortar and point joints.

4 Butter some mortar onto one edge of the first walling block, rest it on the mortar bed and lower it so that it fits into the recess in the pilaster block.

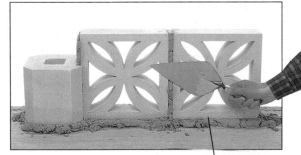

5 Mortar the edge of the next block and place it against its neighbor. Tamp them down gently if necessary to make them level with each other.

The blocks are relatively fragile, so tamp them down only at the corners.

BUILDING A SCREEN WALL

Another effective way of using pierced screen walling blocks is to build areas of blockwork into solid brick or stone walls as decorative infill panels. As the blocks are simply stack-bonded in vertical columns instead of having an interlocking bond like brickwork, a wall more than about two courses high is inherently very weak and could be toppled by high winds. To strengthen a taller wall structure, build the piers around reinforcing rods set in the foundations and reinforce every second course of the wall by bedding a strip of expanded metal mesh in the mortar joint. If the wall is to be more than four courses high, allow the mortar to harden overnight before continuing as described in the panel on the right. The completed wall can be attractively finished with matching pier caps and coping stones.

Building higher walls

If you are building a wall more than two courses high, you must reinforce the piers with a steel rod bedded in the foundations. Bond every other course of blocks to the piers with a strip of expanded metal mesh.

Hook the strip of mesh over the reinforcing rod, press it down into the mortar bed and add a little more mortar on top of it before positioning the next course of blocks.

Lift the next pier block over the top of the reinforcing rod and lower it into position. Make sure as you place it that the slot in which the wall blocks locate is facing the correct way.

Add two more courses of walling blocks and three more pier blocks.

1 If the wall is no higher than two courses of blocks, simply spread a layer of mortar on top of the wall and pier blocks, ready for the pier caps and coping stones.

2 Set the pier cap in place first, checking that it is centered on the pier blocks. Position the first length of coping, butt it up to the pier cap and tamp it down gently.

3 This module illustrates how two wall blocks exactly match the height of three pier blocks. A wall built with pier blocks must have an even number of courses.

Use a pointing trowel to finish off the joints between blocks. Either add more mortar to create flush pointing or draw the trowel along each joint for a sloping joint.

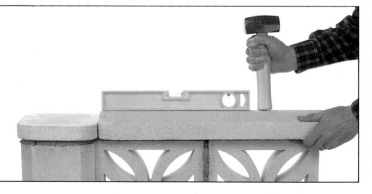

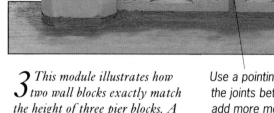

CLIMBING SUPPORT SYSTEMS FOR WALLS

Without adequate support, many climbers produce a disappointing display. You can choose a system that will hardly be seen or a larger scheme that becomes part of your garden design. Trellis panels are effective and relatively easy to fix up, but perhaps the simplest and cheapest support system is to drive small nails or screws into the wall. These have straps or flexible tabs to support and guide the climbing stems as they grow; green plastic ones effectively disappear among the foliage. A more permanent system is an arrangement of horizontal wires stretched across a wall at about 12-inch intervals. Set this up before planting the climber and attach the wires to 'vine eyes' driven or screwed into the brickwork. Such a system allows for all kinds of growth, whether it is fan-shaped or just a simple pillar. Various products are available for tying plant stems to wire or trellis, from soft green string to plastic and paper ties. Check that plants have not outgrown their ties each year and that no string has broken. For scrambling plants, such as clematis, you can buy plastic netting in green, brown or white to match plant or background.

Nail these plant ties directly into bricks or mortar, wrap the long plastic tab around the climber and secure it. These ties can be adjusted and used many times.

You can nail these plastic spacers into the wall to allow air to circulate behind a trellis panel so that water does not collect and degrade the wood.

Small plant supports nailed into the wall close to leading stems encourage them to grow in the right direction and protect them from damage. Bend the soft metal tab over to secure each stem.

These plastic supports are easy to hide among the foliage of climbing plants. Nail them to walls or posts.

Paper-covered wire 'twist-ties' are easy and convenient for 'light duties'. They are also available in plastic.

These traditional style vine eyes can be driven directly into mortar. Thread wire through the small hole ('eye').

These substantial vine eyes can be screwed directly into wooden posts or into plugs inserted in brickwork.

Soft brown string may be less obtrusive than green string in certain situations, and will last one or two seasons.

Soft green string is ideal as a general-purpose 'camouflaged' material for tying up plants.

Garden wire is available in various thicknesses. This green, plastic-covered wire is thin enough to pass through vine eyes and strong enough to support plant growth. On walls, it blends in well with plants and flowers.

Being floppy, plastic clematis netting needs to be well secured all over, including the top and sides, to stop it falling down or blowing around.

TRELLIS OPTIONS

Square trellis looks good on top of a fence or screwed onto walls, where climbers can twine through the spaces. Square trellis can be used horizontally or vertically.

Criss-cross expandable trellis is made of cedar and is excellent for screening unsightly objects. You can alter the shape slightly and use it on walls, either in the horizontal or vertical plane.

For a natural look that complements the plants trained onto them, try a woven-style trellis, such as this panel and the semicircular top section. These are made of malleable willows and hazels and have irregular edges instead of the geometric outlines of conventional panels.

Set in pots, fan-shaped trellis makes an excellent support for climbers. This one has a natural wood finish.

White and green trellis panels are best set against a contrasting background. Screwed on a wall they make stylish backdrops for climbers.

WORKING WITH TRELLIS

As we have seen on page 34, trellis panels are available in a wide variety of styles and materials. Trellis framework is attractive by itself and its impact can be accentuated by painting it in different colors. Natural wood finish and white are favorite options, the latter conveying a 'classic' style to the garden. You can fix trellis panels to free-standing posts to create simple 'walls' that climbers can clothe with foliage and flowers, or you can build up arches, arbors, bowers and pergolas to suit your space and budget. In fact, you can buy many such trellis features as self-assembly kits.

One of the main ways of using trellis panels is to fix them directly to a wall. You can do this simply by drilling through the battens and screwing directly into the brickwork. Do make sure that heavy panels are securely fixed and bear in mind that the climbers will add more weight to the structure. If you are using heavy duty, square mesh trellis you will need to decide whether to place the horizontal or vertical battens closest to the wall. One way might be better for the plants you use.

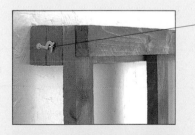

Fix a simple hook-and-eye catch here to secure the panel against the wall.

If you need to remove trellis panels to redecorate the wall, why not hinge them as shown here? Fix them at least 24 inches off the ground so that climbers can flex easily.

Hinge the panel to a batten so that it can swing down from the wall.

Above: *If the horizontal battens are fixed directly against the wall, as here, plant growth may be restricted by the lack of space behind the cross pieces.*

Above right: *Turn the panel round and the cross pieces form a series of 'rungs' on a ladder and are held away from the wall by the vertical battens.*

Right: *To save deciding which way round to fix the panel, you could simply space the whole thing away from the wall by fixing a suitable batten down the sides. This gives plants plenty of room.*

TRELLIS ON THE PATIO

All sorts of interesting effects can be achieved using trellis. Secured to a wall, it supports climbers or wall shrubs and is easy to remove if you need to maintain or paint the wall. As a screen around a patio it provides instant privacy and you can grow climbers on it, either planted in a bed in the ground, or in tubs or troughs on the paving in front of it. You can suspend wall baskets and other hanging containers from it, bolt it to a timber structure or combine it with pergola poles to make an enclosed corner, a shaded area or a romantic, rose-covered arbor. Trellis is best used in reasonably sheltered places. Only the strongest kinds can withstand frequent gale force winds, so make sure that supporting timbers are strong and well secured, and clear away displays of baskets and annual climbers before winter.

Above: Wall-trained shrubs, such as this pyracantha, need support. Trellis is attractive and provides plenty of places to tie back shoots.

Left: A trellis screen is the ideal place to display a collection of wall baskets. Here, all sorts of different plants and containers have been used to create a random, colorful display.

Plastic and wire half baskets are easy to hook onto trellis, and there are plenty of supports available to hang up single pots.

Right: A modern version of the arbor - an enclosed seating area that is quick and easy to erect. The slatted sides provide privacy and shelter, and make a home for plants in wall baskets.

PLANTING A CLIMBING ROSE ON A TRELLIS PANEL

The best time to plant a climbing rose is during the early fall or in the spring. Planting in early fall means that the plant has a few weeks in which to grow and establish itself before the onset of winter. Planting in the spring means that the plant gets off to a quick start and is likely to perform well. Bare-rooted roses tend to be hardier than containerized ones and are therefore better able to cope with the rigors of winter. Containerized roses are available from nurseries or garden centers and can be planted during spring and early summer. Always stand a plant in water for at least ten minutes before planting it. Once established, newly planted climbers and ramblers will need no pruning for at least two years. Simply remove the dead flowers, and in later years, prune out any spindly growth.

1 Dig a planting hole about 12 inches across and deep. Make sure that the hole is at the center of the trellis and not to one side.

4 Use a cane to check the planting depth. Fill in with the soil, mixed with some peat or peat-substitute, plus a slow-release fertilizer.

3 This bare-rooted rose has been pruned back to its three main stems. Position it in the hole, arranging the roots gently and evenly around the base of the hole.

Spread out the branches of the climber and, even though they are short, tie in the shoots to the trellis using soft string and a simple knot.

5 This well-proportioned climbing rose has every prospect of thriving from the good start it has been given. Water it well until established.

2 Fork organic matter into the base of the hole below the plant, where it will not reach the roots. Too much or too fresh manure may 'burn' the roots.

CLEMATIS ON WALLS

Walls are often regarded as the ideal place to grow climbing plants, and clematis have been the first choice for many years. To succeed, it is vital to carry out the initial planting correctly. The base of a wall can be a very dry and inhospitable place and because clematis require more water than the average plant, they often fail when planted in this position, even during the wettest season. It is a good idea to plant the clematis 12–18 inches from the base of the wall and to incorporate plenty of water-retaining material, such as peat. From early spring and right through the growing period, make sure the clematis does not go short of water. Another important consideration is a means of supporting the clematis. There is a wide range of plant supports on the market and your choice is only a matter of personal taste. Alternatively, you can support the clematis with another climber or shrub. This is also a good way of providing protection in winter for a more delicate clematis, such as *Clematis florida* 'Sieboldii', and makes a foil for the flowers.

Trellis for clematis

Hardwood trellis makes a good support for clematis and is widely available in many styles and colors. Clematis need room to attach themselves by their leaf stems, so space the trellis ½ inch away from the wall with pieces of bamboo. Secure the trellis with masonry nails.

Below: A narrow section of hardwood trellis is ideal in a limited space. Grow a compact clematis, such as the 'Comtesse de Bouchaud' shown here.

Above: Hardwood trellis can also be used horizontally. Make sure that the line of the trellis follows that of the bricks, otherwise it looks odd in winter.

Above: If space allows, use a wider section of trellis and a more vigorous clematis or grow more than one variety. Spread out the stems as they grow.

Three trellis panels interlock to form a rigid framework around the drainpipe.

Below: A mix of drainpipe and wall trellis panels make a support that will eventually be covered with a blaze of color.

Left: Here, square mesh wire provides a support for the clematis 'Daniel Deronda'. Attach the wire to the wall with nails.

Plants for patios

If you choose your plants sensibly and tend them carefully, your patio can be the ideal environment they need to flourish. This section provides some valuable advice.

Contents

SUITABLE PLANTS FOR CONTAINERS

It is surprising how many garden plants thrive in containers. Naturally compact kinds look best and naturally drought-tolerant kinds survive best, although even damp-loving plants thrive in containers if kept well watered. For long-lasting displays, choose flowering plants with a long flowering season and foliage plants with really striking foliage. Traditional container planting schemes made up with annual bedding plants are fine for bright spring and summer color, but nowadays people want container plantings that are a bit different.

Many dwarf conifers will turn brown if their roots dry out for any length of time, but the juniper family are much more drought-resistant and will tolerate the occasional dry spell. Dwarf varieties are the most suitable for containers; this Juniperus communis 'Gold Cone' grows to 36 inches high.

Ampelopsis brevipedunculata 'Elegans' is an unusual, small perennial climber for a sheltered spot. The leaves are variegated cream, green and pink.

Houttuynia cordata 'Chameleon' is a first-class container plant. The shoots do not appear above ground until late spring.

Pinks are free-flowering, compact and survive the occasional drying out. Plants are perennial but shortlived; take cuttings in midsummer to replace old plants every three years.

Potentilla fruticosa is a very good compact shrub for containers in a sunny spot, as It tolerates hot conditions. Named varieties are available with pink, yellow, white or red flowers.

Lewisia cotyledon is a particularly drought-proof alpine. It makes a rosette of thick leaves, with salmony pink flowers in early summer.

40

SUITABLE PLANTS FOR CONTAINERS

Now that everyone is busier, the trend is changing towards plants that can stay in the same containers all year round. It can create a more subtle effect, too. You can choose a mixture of small trees, shrubs and ground-covering plants, with herbaceous flowers to create a complete potted garden where there is no flowerbed. If you choose a plant that will grow big, put it in a good-sized container or it will quickly become potbound. Most of the plants used in containers grow best in a warm, sheltered spot, but they may struggle to survive if conditions are too hot, so always ensure that they have enough water.

Good container plants

Compact summer bedding plants, e.g. salvia, petunia, French marigold, lobelia, ageratum.
Pelargonium, fuchsia, gazania, argyranthemums, felicia (bring indoors for the winter).
Winter-flowering pansies, wallflowers, polyanthus, bellis daisies. Spring and summer-flowering bulbs. A selection of herbs, e.g. mint, chervil, parsley. Hostas.
Standard trained wisteria.
Topiary trained box.

Small trees with good foliage add height to a collection of permanent patio plants. Japanese maples, such as this Acer palmatum 'Ornatum', are very attractive.

Large-flowered hybrid clematis are excellent in large containers, but give them a good support. This is 'Elsa Spath'.

Variegated evergreens are particularly valuable in all-year-round planting schemes. Euonymus fortunei varieties, such as this 'Emerald 'n' Gold', make neat compact shapes.

Use containers to grow shrubs that might not otherwise thrive in your garden soil. This Pieris japonica 'Variegata' needs a slightly shaded, sheltered spot with lime-free soil.

Miniature and patio roses are fine for containers, although other roses do not do very well in them. This one is 'Anna Ford'.

UNSUITABLE PLANTS FOR CONTAINERS

Plants with short flowering seasons, a straggly growth habit, uninteresting foliage, tall gangly stems or only one feature of interest instead of several, generally make unexciting subjects for containers. Some plants need putting into the ground soon after you buy them, as they quickly spoil if they are allowed to dry out at the roots. Other plants are unsuitable for long-term growing in containers because they get too big or grow so vigorously that they soon exhaust the limited amount of potting mixture, even in a large container. This is particularly true of climbing roses, cane fruits and large climbers. However, do not be put off using shade and moisture-loving plants – many of them make good container plants, given the right conditions.

Climbing roses do not do well for long in containers and are much more successful if planted in a permanent soil bed near a wall on which you can properly train their branches.

Variegated weeping fig and other tropical foliage plants are easily spoiled in cold and windy, or very sunny conditions.

Some alpines, particularly mossy saxifrages such as this 'Cloth of Gold', scorch badly if they are grown in full sun and allowed to dry out.

Tall herbaceous flowers, such as this lupin, are too top-heavy for a container and lack interest once they have flowered.

Large-flowering houseplants, such as gloxinia, scorch in full sun. Leaves brown if the soil dries out.

UNSUITABLE PLANTS FOR CONTAINERS

This flowering currant has only a short season of interest in spring. Choose a shrub with more variety.

Plants to avoid

Garrya elliptica has brittle roots that dislike being moved. All container plants need repotting every few years to give them fresh soil, so avoid species that do not respond well to this, such as hellebores and euphorbias.

Large trees, including woodland and forest species, are unsuitable for containers unless you train them as bonsai specimens.

Large ornamental trees become potbound and dry out faster than you can water them.

Fruit trees are not ideal in pots, unless grafted onto moderately dwarfing rootstocks and grown in large tubs.

Large untidy or fast-growing shrubs, conifers or flowers soon outgrow their containers.

Avoid plants that cause skin reactions, such as rue and some primulas. Containers are often placed where people brush against them.

Most conifers go brown if they dry out at the roots and the foliage remains brown.

Plants that grow naturally in boggy conditions and need sun, such as this candelabra primula, quickly die if they dry out.

Huge, fast-growing herbs, such as angelica, soon smother other herbs in a tub.

Raspberries, loganberries and the blackberry shown here get far too big, soon exhaust the soil and run out of root room.

Biennial flowers, such as sweet williams, have a shorter flowering time than annuals and are less compact.

CONTAINER PLANTS FOR SHADE

Containers are traditionally associated with sunny sites, but fortunately there are plenty of plants that thrive in a shady corner or in a garden that is entirely in shade. Quite a few plants are fairly easy-going and do well in either sun or partial shade. Others are real shade-lovers and only grow well out of sunlight. This gives you scope either to make the best of a bad job or to take the plunge and create a very 'different' container planting based on true shade-lovers.

A potted shade garden is altogether more subtle than a sunny one, relying on foliage effects and subtle colors for its impact. You could install a small fountain, with or without a pond, to add sparkle to the scene and to reflect light back into the darker areas. And take this opportunity to make the most of variegated plants, shapes and interesting containers and backgrounds to see a shade garden at its best. However, a shade garden need not be without color altogether. Plenty of plants provide seasonal flowers throughout most of the year.

One potential problem in shady gardens – even more so than in sunny ones – is that of slugs and snails. They thrive in the cool, moist shade under plants and find the thin leaves of hostas and toad lilies particularly to their liking. If you do not like using slug pellets, mulching containers and beds with cocoa-shell seems to deter them.

Hardy ferns are fantastic foliage plants for shade. Keep them moist. This evergreen *Phyllitis scolopendrium* 'Cristata' is the curly hart's tongue fern.

Hydrangeas do well in containers in a shaded spot, given plenty of moisture. Leave the dead flowerheads on over winter to protect young shoots, then prune them back in spring to where they join a young branch. This lacecap variety has sterile florets in the center that never open.

Hostas of all sorts make superb plants for containers and look 'at home' in light shade. They will also grow in sunnier spots, given plenty of water.

Begonia semperflorens thrives in shade if you delay planting it until it has started flowering.

Specialist growers advertise a range of unusual variegated and curly- or narrow-leaved ivies.

CONTAINER PLANTS FOR SHADE

A dwarf rhododendron makes a good spring display in a large tub. Plant it in a mixture of half ericaceous and half soil-based potting mix.

This alpine strawberry thrives in shade under other plants. The tiny, edible fruits are delicious.

Plants for shade

Rhododendrons, camellias and pieris. Asiatic and oriental hybrid lilies. Toad lilies (*Tricyrtis*). Hardy cyclamen. *Oxalis triangularis* 'Atropurpurea'. Mophead and lacecap hydrangeas. Foxgloves. Compact, shade-loving herbaceous plants - *Pulmonaria*, variegated brunnera, *Alchemilla mollis*, *Lunaria annua* 'Variegata'. *Acer palmatum* and cultivars (Japanese maple). *Fatsia japonica*, *Aucuba japonica*. Box (clipped topiary).

Unlike most annuals that need plenty of sun, impatiens are useful for providing color in shady areas.

Above: Hardy ferns and hostas are fashionable and collectable plants for a shady spot. They associate together very well and thrive in containers. Do watch out for watering, as these plants need to be moist at all times.

Low, ground-covering perennials with good foliage are useful in all-year-round plantings. This Ajuga reptans 'Braunherz' has shiny purplish black leaves.

THE PATIO IN SPRING

Even though it may be too cold to sit outside in spring, the patio is still visible from indoors and a colorful display of flowers is welcome at the end of a long winter. Good plants for spring displays include bulbs - daffodils, hyacinths, tulips, etc. - and flowers such as polyanthus, wallflowers, forget-me-nots, stocks and double bellis daisies. In mild areas, you can plant these out in the fall after removing the summer annuals. However, in spring, you may find a wider range of plants and as they have not weathered the winter outdoors, they will probably be in better shape than those planted out in the fall. Harden them off in a cold frame or stand them outside during the day and bring them in at night for a week or so before planting. Choose plants in tight bud to give them time to adjust to the conditions before the flower opens.

Bulbs in containers

Choose compact bulb varieties and soil-based potting mix or reuse the soil in summer tubs. Plant the bulbs close together but not quite touching and cover them with twice their own depth of soil. Fill the container to the rim with soil, water it lightly and put it in a cool place. When the tips of the shoots show through, move the bulbs to the patio. Protect from excess rain or bulbs may rot.

Skimmia japonica 'Rubella'. These are the tight flowerbuds of this male-only form. They open to white in spring. The pollen can fertilize the flowers of female-only forms, such as 'Foremanni'.

Narcissus 'Tête-à-Tête'

Left: A combination of spring flowers and bulbs with berrying and budding skimmias. A male and female variety are included so that the female plant produces berries.

Skimmia japonica 'Foremanni'. This form has female flowers only. When planted with a male form, such as 'Rubella', it produces these vivid red berries.

Polyanthus

Variegated ivy (Hedera helix cultivar)

BULBS FOR COLORFUL SPRING DISPLAYS

Rather than leave containers empty in winter, why not plant bulbs? All you need are durable, weatherproof containers. Wood, stone and good-quality plastics are all suitable for outdoor winter use and frostproof terracotta and ceramic pots are available, too. Most bulbs can be planted in the early fall, although tulips are late-rooting and best not planted until mid-fall. Once planted, water the containers lightly and protect them from excess rain until the young shoots start to appear. For winter color, plant the bulbs with ivies, euonymus or other small evergreens.

Do not keep tubs of bulbs in the greenhouse until they are in flower and then expect them to survive outdoors. Instead, move tubs to their display positions as soon as the first green shoots appear so that the emerging plants will be hardened to the conditions by the time the flowers appear. You can buy bulbs growing in pots in garden centers in spring. Often, they coincide with other spring bedding, so it is easy to put together an instant display.

When planting bulbs from pots, avoid disturbing the rootball; this can give them such a check that they do not flower properly or the leaves start to turn yellow. It is often easier to plunge pots of bulbs up to the rim into an existing display.

Below: Formal-looking hybrid tulips look best in formal containers with a symmetrical planting scheme.

Above: Bulbs in pots, such as these hyacinths, can be brought indoors when the buds are showing their true color. Stand them in a plastic-lined basket surrounded by moss to hide the pots.

Left: Paperwhite narcissi planted with polyanthus and winter-flowering pansies.

The feet underneath the pot raise it up just enough to provide better drainage.

THE PATIO IN SUMMER

Summer is the patio season: bedding plants, summer-flowering bulbs, patio roses, dwarf shrubs, herbs and perennials all contribute to a riot of color. Choose a mixture of colors or a scheme based on one or two colors for a more sophisticated effect. Decide whether you want strong contrasts or a gentle harmonizing effect. Bright colors stand out best against a contrasting background; in containers you can achieve these effects by teaming bright flowers with colored foliage plants, such as coleus and purple-leaved basil. For a harmonious effect, use similar colored flowers and foliage together – blue, purple and mauve or shades of pink and red. Color can also create an atmosphere. A 'hot' scheme of red, yellow and orange looks tropical and busy, while cool green and white or blue and mauve are relaxing. Play with color to make a small patio look bigger. Bright red and yellow plants in the foreground give the impression that they are very close to you. Muted mauves and misty purples at the other end of the patio give the impression of distance.

Left: Impatiens *are good-value bedding plants that stay in flower all through the summer. They are most impressive when planted in large groups. Unlike most bedding plants, they will continue to flower happily, even when they are in a shady spot.*

Right: A 'cameo' of climbing roses, summer-flowering lilies, Phormium *(New Zealand flax)* and Convolvulus cneorum *(at the bottom lefthand corner of the picture). The ornamental trellis acts as a frame for the container.*

HERBACEOUS PLANTS FOR A STYLISH PATIO

Herbaceous plants make a pleasant change from annuals for stylish patio planting. With them, you can recreate a traditional herbaceous border in miniature, or cool, sophisticated schemes based on foliage and flowers. Some herbaceous plants are very suitable for growing in containers – *Houttuynia cordata* 'Chameleon', agapanthus, hostas and *Hakonechloa macra* 'Albo-aurea' are all good – but most fairly compact kinds can be grown in this way, given adequate moisture. The easiest way to grow herbaceous plants is in beds, and a bed next to a patio wall or sunk into paving provides a warm, sheltered situation for some of the more heat-loving kinds. Moisture-loving species will grow in any bed that does not dry out.

Herbaceous plants for all sites and seasons

In hot spots: hemerocallis, scabiosa, verbascum, dictamnus (burning bush), *Sedum spectabile*, euphorbia, agapanthus, alchemilla, limonium, incarvillea, stachys and artemisia. Moisture-loving species: astilbe, hosta, lysimachia, trollius (globe flower), zantedeschia (arum lily), and mimulus (musk). For spring color: pulmonaria (lungwort), brunnera, bergenia and dicentra. For late summer and fall color: phlox, Japanese anemones, perennial asters, hardy chrysanthemums, penstemon, rudbeckia, schizostylis, *Liriope muscari* and phygelius (Cape figwort).

Left: African lilies (Agapanthus) are excellent for containers and appreciate the warmth and shelter of a patio. In winter, lag the pots or move them to a cold greenhouse to protect the plant roots.

Hosta foliage lasts well all season. The plants produce spikes of pale pink flowers in midsummer.

Below: Hostas are highly underrated as container plants. Growing them in pots makes it harder for slugs to find their juicy leaves and nibble at them.

A SELECTION OF PATIO ROSES

The very best kinds of roses for pots are patio and miniature varieties, which normally grow 1–3 feet tall. Choose 10-inch pots for miniatures, 12-inch pots for patio roses and 15-inch or even larger pots for compact hybrid teas and floribundas. You can grow the roses in clay or plastic flowerpots, in ornamental tubs or half barrels, but avoid shallow troughs. Fill containers with good-quality, soil-based potting mixture. Being low-growing, miniature and patio roses also thrive in raised beds on the patio. You can plant roses in spring or in summer while they are in flower, but do not disturb the rootball. Keep the containers well fed and watered - use a liquid tomato feed at half strength or a liquid rose feed. Do not let the soil dry out, and deadhead the flowers regularly so that new ones are constantly produced from early summer until the fall. Repot container roses into the same pot but with fresh potting mixture every two years at pruning time.

Pruning a miniature rose

Most miniature roses are grown from cuttings, which means that they grow on their own roots and must be cut back quite severely every spring. The prunings can be used to make new plants. Pruning a miniature rose may seem to be an irksome task, but the results of cleaning up and cutting back quite hard are well worthwhile. Miniature roses grown in containers also benefit from annual repotting.

The scented, bicolored flowers appear all summer long.

Left: *'Buffalo Bill' (also known as 'Regensberg' or 'Young Mistress') is a compact red-and-white floribunda rose suitable for growing in a large patio pot.*

Above: *'Orange Masquerade' is a patio rose that makes a good neat shape in a container. It will produce these intensely colored flowers throughout the summer.*

STANDARD FUCHSIAS

Fuchsias look wonderful grown as standards; elevated on a stem you can enjoy the beauty of their flowers and their elegance so much more. It is an ideal way of looking at fuchsias with upright flowers. The basic requirements for growing a standard are a good, straight stem, a well-formed head and a good covering of flowers. Use a trailing cultivar and you will have a lovely weeping standard. You can grow any variety as a standard, although some will require much more effort than others. Never grow a standard that will be taller than you can easily manage to keep through the winter. Be wary of proportion; a large flower on a short standard will look odd, as will a small head on a long stem. Small flowers on small standards look much better. Always bring standard fuchsias into a frost-free place for the winter months in cool temperate climates, otherwise you could end up with a bush rather than a standard. The stem can easily be caught by a cold spell, as there is no protection for it. All it needs to survive the winter is a warmer environment.

Best cultivars

Singles: Alison Patricia, Celia Smedley, Chang, Checkerboard, Estelle Marie, Jenny Sorenson, Joy Patmore, Olive Smith, Reg Gubler,
Doubles: Annabel, Brookwood Bell, Cotton Candy, Dancing Flame, Happy Wedding Day, King's Ransom, Swingtime.

Right: Shelford has been one of the most popular cultivars during the last few years. It flowers continuously for many months and is easy to shape. The shadier the planting position, the whiter the flowers will be. In a sunny spot, the flowers are almost pink.

Right: Royal Velvet is a fine old cultivar. The weight of the large double flowers gives it an almost weeping shape. This type of growth may need extra support, such as tying the branches to a central cane.

FLOWERING SHRUBS FOR THE PATIO

Shrubs can be grown in containers or in beds in the ground, but as space is limited, choose reasonably compact kinds that have particularly attractive or, better still, evergreen foliage, a long flowering season, or fruit and flowers. Or team very compact shrubs with other small flowering plants in, say, a rock garden. Drought-resistant shrubs are good in small containers or in a hot, dry spot between paving. Shrubs can make a low-maintenance, year-round background to containers of flowering plants or they can be the center of interest in their own right. You could plan a bed with one striking plant, such as a patio rose, as the centerpiece and smaller bulbs or ground-hugging plants growing around it. Look for roses that have been grafted onto a tall stem to give a weeping effect, such as 'Nozomi'.

Alternatively, put together a group of shrubs of contrasting colors, shapes and sizes for the best effect. And look out for little-known but spectacular flowering shrubs that will thrive in the sun and shelter of a patio.

Left: *In a sheltered spot close to a house, camellias flower a little earlier and the lovely flowers are less likely to be spoiled by bad weather.*

Right: *A fringe of evergreen shrubs around the patio provides all-year-round privacy and shelter. When not in flower, these rhododendrons provide a superb background for other colorful plants in containers.*

A flowering patio

Ballerina apple tree 'Maypole'
Callistemon citrinus (bottlebrush)
Camellias (any)
Ceratostigma willmottianum (hardy plumbago)
Fabiana imbricata
Hebe
Hibiscus syriacus
Hydrangeas
Indigofera heterantha
Olearia haastii (daisy bush)
Potentilla
Prunus incisa (Fuji cherry) - try 'Kojo no Mai', a naturally dwarf form 3-4-foot high
Dwarf rhododendron

Above: *Dwarf rhododendrons, such as 'Elizabeth', make good permanent patio subjects in large tubs with ericaceous potting mix.*

HEATHERS AND CONIFERS

1 Select the heathers and a couple of dwarf conifers - an upright and a domed variety look good in a mixed planting scheme.

The heathers need ericaceous potting mix, which suits the conifers, too.

Evergreen plants are ideal as the basis of easy-care but stunning all-year-round patio displays, as they look good all the time but need minimum maintenance. Some of the most suitable subjects include dwarf conifers, heathers and grassy plants. You could also add very compact evergreen shrubs, such as variegated euonymus, for variety and tuck in a few small spring bulbs or alpines for seasonal interest. Bear in mind the growth rates of the plants. A large mixed tub can soon look unbalanced if some subjects 'take over', so always check how big and how fast you can expect everything to grow. Check, too, for soil requirements. Many heathers, for example, must have a lime-free potting mix. Conifers and many evergreen shrubs will be happy in this, too, but some evergreen shrubs, such as box, prefer normal soil, so do not plant them in the same container.

4 The finished display should last for several years before the plants get too big and need replacing. Clip heathers after flowering and water in dry spells.

2 Almost fill the tub with potting mix and arrange the plants. The upright conifer will look best towards the back of the display.

3 Tap the plants out of their pots and put them as close together as possible, so that the tub is well filled and looks instantly mature. Variegated evergreens add more interest.

Erica tetralix 'Pink Star'

Acorus gramineus 'Ogon'

Chamaecyparis thyoides 'Ericoides'

Juniperus communis 'Compressa'

Erica cinerea 'Katinka'

Erica vagans 'St Keverne'

Euonymus fortunei 'Harlequin'

ROCK PLANTS ON THE PATIO

Rock plants make good subjects for patio containers. Neat, compact and often more drought-tolerant than bedding plants, alpines are also very collectable. When buying rock plants for a patio, make sure that the kinds you have chosen will suit the conditions. Although many enjoy plenty of sun, warmth and dry air, not all are so easy to please. Some, such as ramonda, need cool, shady conditions; lithospermum and some gentians need lime-free soil, while campanulas and the gentians need to be shaded from searing sun, and moist but open-textured soil from which surplus water can drain quickly. The most drought-tolerant rock plants are those with thick succulent leaves, but others with silver leaves, or narrow hard foliage, such as thymes and helianthemum, are good, too. These types of rock plant grow best in terracotta pots and troughs, but provided they are not overwatered or allowed to stand waterlogged in winter, they grow equally well in plastic containers.

Right: Genuine old stone sinks are popular for alpine plants, but are scarce and expensive. Cheaper copies made from cement are now available. Ensure that there are drainage holes and put 1-2 inches of gravel in the bottom before filling with a soil-based mix with extra grit to improve drainage.

Right: A collection of drought-proof alpines in pots is a good way of decorating steps. Here, sempervivums (houseleeks) flourish in terracotta containers. These plants are available in hundreds of varieties.

Houseleek
(Sempervivum)

Potentilla
verna

Picea glauca
'Albertiana
Conica'

Oxalis sp.

Lewisia
cotyledon

Draba sp.

Juniperus
'Blue Star'

Gentian

Aubretia

Saxifrages

CREATIVE ALPINE DISPLAYS

You can create most attractive displays by grouping together three or five containers of alpines. (Odd numbers always look best.) For the best effect, choose similar containers of different sizes, each planted with alpines that grow at roughly the same rate and share similar growing requirements. Alternatively, you could team a sink garden with one large or several smaller pots of alpines. Alpine containers also look superb on paving with ground-hugging alpines planted in the cracks between the slabs. An alpine container garden is an ideal way of housing a collection of interesting plants without taking up a lot of space, but bear in mind that alpines need regular attention to look their best. Water them during dry spells, as the soil should never dry out completely. A layer of grit chippings over the soil surface, tucked in well around the necks of the plants, helps prevent rotting. Remove dead flowers and leaves to prevent pests and diseases from gaining a foothold. Every three years or so, remove all the plants, divide or replace them with new ones and replant the container with fresh potting mix and grit.

Left: Saxifraga oppositifolia *'Splendens' is a ground-hugging 'treasure' that flowers in early spring. For the rest of the year, the carpet of tiny, silver-tipped rosettes makes a useful 'foil' to later flowers. Provide well-drained soil, but do not allow the plant to dry out completely.*

Right: This large area of paving has been broken up by a rocky 'outcrop' - four stone butler's sinks amid a rock garden of dwarf conifers for year-round interest.

Below: A pair of sinks, raised up so that the larger one is slightly higher, makes a pleasing arrangement, together with pans of smaller plants in typical rock plant surroundings - paving, gravel and a background of small, choice, sun-loving plants.

You can make these troughs out of hypertufa

PLANTED POTS GALORE

A patio certainly would not look right without potted plants, but containers can be used in many more ways, all around the garden. You can use a group of them, in different sizes, to decorate a large expanse of hard surfacing, such as a path or driveway. Stand them next to doors or gates for emphasis, or next to seats to provide close detail by way of contrast with a more distant view. Entrances are an ideal place for tubs of scented plants, but make sure that the size of the container and the entrance are in scale with each other. Containers can solve certain gardening problems. For example, if your border develops a gap later in the season, you can stand a container of flowering plants on the spot. If the ground is soft, lay a small paving slab on the soil as a firm base for the pot. Containers are a good way of introducing instant color to an area in need of a quick 'lift'. And use them to camouflage drain covers. A container big enough to sit over the top is perfect; choose a slightly squat one, so that when filled with plants and potting mix it is not too heavy to move if you need to get at the plumbing below.

Right: Nicotianas and Begonia semperflorens *team up in this low terracotta container to provide a dazzling display of sharp pinks and reds.*

Below: A tall terracotta pot lifts its cargo of tulips well above the level of the surrounding spring border, making them stand out. A low-growing garden, such as one specially for herbs, can be given some height with tall containers.

Above: A pot of thymes looks quite at home on a rustic seat. The fragrant leaves and flowers of these useful herbs are ideal for containers.

Water features

A patio pool adds a new dimension, giving you the opportunity to grow exciting plants and to enjoy the sight and sounds of moving water. This section opens the door to that new world.

Contents

Below: This two-level pool links the patio to the garden without looking over formal.

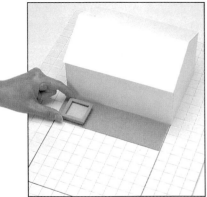

Experiment with overlapping and interlocking shapes when planning formal pools. Always plan and construct a pool with care. Once established, a well-planned pool or water feature will be easier to maintain.

Left: Design a patio pool to fit the shape and size of an existing paved area, and raise it up if excavation work is not practical.

PLANNING A PATIO POOL

It is important to position a pool carefully within the plot and to consider the practical implications, as well as the design possibilities. Water and water plants need plenty of light and sunshine, so avoid a shady spot. Try not to position a pool too near to trees, as falling leaves can pollute the water, or too close to a boundary, where there could be construction and maintenance problems. For an informal, natural pool sketch out a rough kidney shape without too many inlets, as these are difficult to construct. Alternatively, choose a more formal square, rectangle or circle, which could be raised or sunk into the ground. You might even consider two or more pools linked by a water spout or cascade to produce a change of level on the patio or to link patio to garden.

Using concrete

Some people still favor concrete for lining a pool. It is certainly strong and can be watertight providing it is correctly mixed and applied. Concreting a pool is not a job for a novice. Even the simplest design will need to incorporate some reinforcing material. The components must be kept clean and be accurately measured, and the work carried out when there is no risk of frost or extremely dry, sunny weather.

Installing a raised pool

The big advantage of a raised pool is that there is no digging and relatively little disturbance to the patio. You can easily integrate a raised pool with other features, such as seating and raised beds. There may be practical reasons why a raised pool is preferable: a difficult site with bedrock just below the surface; a high water table; a sloping site or simply a small budget. If you want to make a raised pool using a liner or a preformed unit, it is best to choose a circular or oval shape to help the pool withstand the pressure of water; without the support of soil around it, a square-edged design would be prone to splitting or breaking down at the corners. On a formal patio, you can edge the pool with pavers or brick to match the patio, and remember that the wide rim of coping stones makes a handy place to sit and admire the sound and sparkle of the water or to stand pots of suitable plants.

Above: A formal raised pool with a fountain makes a fine focal point to the patio.

AQUATIC BASKETS, LINERS AND SOIL

Water plants can be planted directly into the soil or mulch at the bottom of the pool or on the marginal shelf. However, with smaller pools, using special rot-proof plastic pots and containers makes the plants – and pond – much easier to handle. A wide range of containers is available, their sides perforated to keep the soil moist and aerated. Baskets tend to have a wide base to make them stable and are usually black, which makes them virtually invisible once they are in the water. Large–weave baskets need lining with hessian or woven plastic material to prevent the soil washing away, but the containers with a close–weave pattern do not need lining. The soil you use for aquatic plants should be a rich and heavy loam to ensure that it has plenty of nutrients and remains waterlogged. A clay soil has the right consistency, but is usually not rich enough. Sandy or chalky soils are too fine and will wash out of the containers. Make sure that any soil you use is free from any potentially harmful chemicals or herbicides.

Aquatic soil

You can buy special potting mixtures recommended for water plants from garden centers and aquatic specialists. Avoid general garden potting mixtures, as these contain peat (too acidic for most aquatic plants) and soluble fertilizers. Never use fertilizers or rotted manure in the pool as they encourage the growth of algae.

Glyceria spectabilis 'Variegata', an attractively striped grass that grows about 24 inches high.

Square fine-meshed basket for large marginals.

Hydrocotyle vulgaris, a low-growing marginal, produces delicate nodding blooms.

The marsh marigold, Caltha palustris, is a popular and dependable marginal plant.

These marginal baskets are designed to take a selection of plants and are curved to fit the edge of a circular or other informal shape of pool.

Large-weave plastic container for lilies and marginals.

Circular baskets with louvered sides and fine perforations are ideal for lilies and larger marginal plants. They do not need lining.

A small planting pot with fine mesh panels.

Hessian lining material.

Plastic liner for large mesh containers.

Water-retaining potting mixture formulated for aquatic plants.

Small stones, pebbles or gravel as a topdressing to retain soil in containers.

Mimulus luteus 'Nana', an attractive marginal plant.

OXYGENATING PLANTS

A selection of oxygenating plants is essential for the good health of your pond, especially if it is new. These are mostly submerged, or occasionally floating, species of water plants that use up waste nutrients in the water by means of their underwater foliage. They quickly deprive bothersome algae of nutrients and minerals, and thus help to keep the water clean. Few oxygenators are as pretty as the water violet, *Hottonia palustris*, which produces a mass of pale mauve flowers above a dense underwater mat of fernlike foliage, but they generally do their job well, not only preventing green water and blanketweed, but also providing useful cover for pond life. For the average pool, you will need about one oxygenating plant for every 2 square feet of surface area. Larger pools, over 150 square feet can reduce that requirement to nearer one plant per 3 square feet. Different species flourish at different times of year, so a selection of two or three is the most successful way to beat murky water.

Evergreen Fontinalis antipyretica *thrives in sun or semi-shade and prefers running water, such as a stream.*

Eleocharis acicularis, *or hairgrass, is an evergreen sedge that spreads prolifically to produce a dense mat of narrow green leaf spikes.*

Hottonia palustris, *or water violet, makes a clump of feathery, light green leaves, with tall spikes of flowers.*

Ranunculus aquatilis, *the water buttercup, has bright green feathery foliage that can be invasive if not kept in check.*

The tiny, semi-evergreen leaves of Lagarosiphon major *(also known as Elodea crispa) are clustered along each stem.*

Hardy Ceratophyllum demersum, *or hornwort, grows best in cool water, where it spreads to make a submerged mat of tiny dark green leaves.*

Oxygenators

Callitriche hermaphroditica
(C. autumnalis)
Callitriche palustris (C. verna)
Ceratophyllum demersum
Crassula recurva
Eleocharis acicularis
Fontinalis antipyretica
Hottonia palustris
Lagarosiphon major
(Elodea crispa)
Myriophyllum proserpinacoides
Myriophyllum verticillatum
Potamogeton crispus
Ranunculus aquatilis

60

PLANTING A MARGINAL

Marginal plants will thrive with their roots submerged in water but their foliage must be free of the water surface. Plant them quickly, so that their roots and stems are exposed for as short a time as possible, and plant them at exactly the same level as they were in the pot or nursery bed. Remove the plants carefully from their container, but not until you have everything ready to plant, otherwise the roots may suffer. If you have a 'natural' pond with soil submerged around the edges, you can plant directly on the marginal shelf by backfilling with a suitably rich, water-retaining soil. Hold the plants in place with large rocks or boulders. For pools with 'clean' marginal shelves you can use special containers that you can lower onto the shelf and lift out for easy maintenance. These containers are available in various sizes suited to single specimens or several plants together. Curved baskets are ideal for the marginal shelf around a circular pool.

2 Remove the marginal plant gently from its pot, taking care to support the stem loosely between your fingers.

3 Carefully position two or three plants of the same species in the container for a good display. Backfill and firm in.

4 Finish filling the container with aquatic soil and level the surface. Add a layer of gravel so that the soil does not float away.

1 Once you have assembled all the materials and plants you need, you can begin filling the marginal basket with moist aquatic potting soil.

Keep the plants moist and in their original pots until you use them.

Make sure that the topdressing of gravel is clean and washed.

The marginal basket is in position on the shelf with the plants visible from the pool edge. It is easy to lift the container out for maintenance.

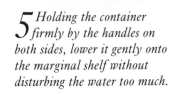

5 Holding the container firmly by the handles on both sides, lower it gently onto the marginal shelf without disturbing the water too much.

MOISTURE-LOVING PLANTS

Iris sibirica
'Sparkling Rose'

Below: The subtle hues of four plants suitable for moist soil. The Iris *and* Peltiphyllum *will even thrive in boggy conditions.*

Peltiphyllum peltatum

Aquilegia alpina

Geranium sanguineum *'Glenluce'*

Moisture-loving plants are ideal for maintaining that poolside look, where there may not be a natural wet edge - in patio gardens, for example, or where the pond has a butyl or concrete liner. Because most of them grow prolifically given the right conditions, and as the majority have striking flowers or foliage (or both), they are an eye-catching part of the feature and have a wonderful softening effect on pond or stream edges, even in a patio location. To create the right effect around a small patio pond surrounded by paving, you can plant several of these lush species in pots or containers and position them in close groups near the water. Keep the containers well watered and mulch them in dry weather. Where you do have access to soil or planting beds, make sure that the soil is rich in humus to keep it damp and mulch it well to prevent moisture loss. If you cannot keep the soil damp, choose plants that tolerate drier conditions.

Below: Primulas flower mainly in late spring and early summer. Provide them with soil that never dries out, and sun or slight shade, depending on species. The plant care label will give details.

Primula japonica

Primula japonica 'Postford White'

Primula pulverulenta

Primula veris (cowslip)

Primula x 'Geisha Girl'

Primula chungensis

Primula vulgaris flore plena *'Dawn Ansell'*

SMALL WATER LILIES

For many pond owners, the water lily is the epitome of a water garden. There is a wonderful variety of types, offering different colors, forms, foliage and even scent. Choose varieties with care, as the large vigorous types are totally unsuitable for smaller pools. For the smallest ponds there are miniature lilies with a spread of about 12 square inches, and these need a depth of water of only 4–9 inches. Slightly larger, and ideal for small to medium-sized pools, is the group classified as 'small lilies,' with a spread of up to 3 square feet. They require a planting depth of 6–15 inches. These smaller types will grow on the marginal shelf or in plastic baskets, but make sure that the crown is well below ice level to prevent frost damage. Miniature varieties will need adequate protection in winter in cold climates. Whatever the size of the pool, water lilies serve a practical purpose as well as a decorative one; the spread of their leaves covers a large part of the water surface, offering shade and shelter for fish and depriving algae of sunlight. Without light and heat, the algae cannot reproduce too rapidly and give you problems with green water.

Left: The open cup, faintly scented 3½-inch flowers of Nymphaea 'Indiana' darken as they age to a deep apricot orange and finally red. The leaves are marbled with dark brown.

Other small lilies

pygmaea 'Alba' (white)
'Laydekeri Liliacea' (pink)
'Laydekeri Purpurata' (red)
pygmaea 'Rubra' (red)
candida (white)
'Ellisiana' (red), 'Froebeli' (red)
'Aurora' (copper yellow turning to salmon orange, then red)
'Robinsoniana' (vermilion/orange)

Right: The hardy Nymphaea x laydekeri 'Fulgens' produces brilliant red, star-shaped blooms in summer, each one measuring 2–4 inches across.

Below: Nymphaea odorata minor. The sweetly scented flowers, up to 3½ inches across in size, are borne from mid- to late summer above plain green foliage.

63

1 *If there is not already a natural depression in the ground, begin by excavating the area to a depth of about 14 inches.*

Roughly level the base of the hole and ensure that there are no large stones or sharp objects in the soil that might puncture the liner.

2 *Spread the area with a large sheet of pond lining material. Use butyl rubber or the cheaper PVC-based type of liner.*

CREATING A BOG GARDEN OR MARSH AREA

In the ideal bog garden, there should be water standing about 2 inches on the top. You must keep the area poorly drained and make allowances for fluctuations in the water level throughout the year. In a naturally boggy site this is not a problem, but where you have created the environment artificially, you will need some kind of overflow facilities. This is easily installed where the bog garden adjoins a pool area by providing a few holes (about ½ inch in diameter) in the dividing wall. For this two-way top-up drainage system to work, the bog area should represent no more than about ten to fifteen percent of the total surface area of the pond. If there is no pond next to the bog garden, then you can install overflow facilities into a nearby ditch. The easiest way to top up the moisture levels in a dry spell is to insert a length of punctured plastic pipe at the construction stage. If you conceal the exposed end of the pipe among the plants in the bog garden you can trickle in more water when required.

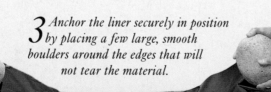

3 *Anchor the liner securely in position by placing a few large, smooth boulders around the edges that will not tear the material.*

4 *Puncture the bottom of the liner a couple of times, so that some of the water can escape later on. Add a layer of washed gravel.*

5 *Lay a section of perforated pipe on the gravel. Extend the end of the pipe beyond the bog area and conceal it in the plants.*

6 *With the pipe in place, fill the area to the original ground level with a rich, moisture-retaining aquatic planting mix.*

7 *Soak the ground thoroughly, so that about 3 inches of water remains standing on the top of the soil before you put in any plants.*

PLANTING UP THE BOG GARDEN

The beauty of a bog or marsh area is that it offers you the chance to grow a wider range of marginal plants. Here we show how to plant up the bog garden created on page 64. If your garden is small or unsuitable, you can still enjoy a miniature bog garden created in an old stone sink or barrel, providing there are three or four drainage holes and a good layer of crocks in the bottom. You can grow one or two moisture-loving plants in each container as long as you keep the soil saturated; mulching with pebbles helps to reduce moisture loss. The containers can stand on the patio or in the garden; a series of tubs containing different plants and sunk to their rims in a bed of gravel looks particularly effective.

Or arrange several old sinks on the patio at various levels.

3 Some marginals, such as this hosta, offer wonderful shape and color possibilities in their foliage. Protect them from slugs and snails.

4 In extremely dry conditions, top up the water level using the piece of pipe you inserted at the construction stage.

1 When the soil is saturated, you can start to add a selection of suitable bog garden plants. There is plenty of choice.

2 Position the plants in the ground so that they are at the same depth as they were in their pots. Firm them in well.

Lysimachia thyrsiflora

Lobelia cardinalis

Hosta

Astilbe

Primula veris

Mimulus

5 Aim for a variety of shape, size and color in your plants to produce an eye-catching show throughout the growing season.

Pipe left accessible for watering

CREATING A WATER FEATURE IN A BARREL

If you are really pressed for space, you can always set up a miniature pool in a pot, tub or other suitable container. Providing they are scaled down, you can have all the features you set your heart on - plants, fish and even a tiny sparkling fountain - and the finished tub can be a real focal point. Any waterproof container is suitable, from a large cut-down barrel to a small terracotta or plastic patio pot. The only real proviso is that it has not been treated with any poisonous or fungicidal chemicals that might damage plants and fish. Some garden centers sell tub kits that come complete with everything you need, even a selection of plants, to be assembled at home. Alternatively, buy a ready-made bubble fountain in a stone or terracotta container, with plants and pebbles installed for an instant moving water feature.

1 Waterproof the barrel by pushing a large piece of pond liner firmly down inside it. Trim off some of the excess at this stage, but leave plenty around the edges to allow for it to settle down further as you add water and bricks.

2 Put the water pump in now. This is a small, mains-powered model ideally suited to the size of the display. Place it on a brick for stability and to bring it up to the correct height.

3 Place a layer of bricks around the inside of the barrel. These will provide platforms to support the plant pots and stones. Use hard bricks sold for paving; they are more durable in water.

4 Add some cobbles to fill in the spaces between the bricks. These will help to stabilize the piles of bricks and will also stop the pump moving around once the feature is operating.

5 Now add the large stones that will form the visible part of the feature. Rounded boulders such as these not only look attractive but will also stand continuous immersion in water.

6 Add water until it reaches the base of the boulders. This will leave enough expansion room to add the plants and final stones.

PLANTING UP THE BARREL

Here we show how to plant up the barrel prepared on page 66. Of course, all kinds of troughs, pots, tubs and barrels are suitable for planting up in this way as long as they are painted inside with a sealant or lined with butyl rubber or plastic pond liner to ensure that they are watertight. Do remember that once filled with water, a few plants and an ornament or fountain, the tub is going to be extremely heavy, so decide on its final position while it is empty and plant it up in situ. If you are going to have to move the feature, place the container on a low platform with lockable casters for mobility. A water feature in a tub makes an excellent focal point for a dull corner of the patio, where it might be raised on such a platform or a few bricks for extra prominence. Alternatively, stand it on a bed of pebbles or gravel or surround it with large stones and pots of lush plants.

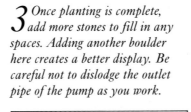

3 Once planting is complete, add more stones to fill in any spaces. Adding another boulder here creates a better display. Be careful not to dislodge the outlet pipe of the pump as you work.

4 Add cobbles and pebbles to match the color range and shape of the boulders. This helps the feature to look more like the bank of a natural stream.

Lysimachia thyrsiflora

Ranunculus flammula

Iris versicolor 'Blue Light'

Myosotis palustris

1 If you want to neaten things up a bit at this stage you can trim off more of the liner. The weight of the water will have pushed the liner into its final position.

2 Now begin to add the plants. Since they will be immersed in water, you can choose from a wide range of exciting marginal plants that thrive in these conditions. Pot them into the plastic mesh baskets made for ponds.

Troughs and windowboxes

These containers typically overflow with summer color, but they are more versatile than you might at first imagine. This section offers some fresh alternatives to the accepted view.

Contents

WONDERFUL WINDOWBOXES

Windowboxes must look their best all the time, so they need careful planning and regular replanting. They are normally planted with seasonal flowers and although it means more work, a series of fresh displays looks much more interesting in such a highly visible situation. Choose pot-grown plants already in flower, as they give an instant effect. The most suitable plants for windowboxes are the compact kinds that flower continuously over a fairly long season. You can mix together annuals as you would in normal containers; herbs make another good summer display. Evergreens, such as dwarf conifers or ivies, can be used temporarily as foliage to accompany flowering plants in windowboxes, but do not leave them in for more than a year, as they soon grow too large. Tip out windowboxes every year in spring, just before planting summer bedding, refill them with fresh potting mix and trim or replace overgrown foliage plants.

Below: These impatiens are ideal for a windowbox that does not get much sun. They actually prefer light dappled shade. If the plants are in flower at the time of planting, they will carry on.

Left: This symmetrical display features Grevillea *for central foliage,* Begonia semperflorens, *ivy-leaved pelargoniums and* Helichrysum 'Limelight'.

Right: For maximum impact, fill the windowbox full of plants. Ivy-leaved and zonal pelargoniums provide the main display, with Argyranthemum *buds waiting to come out and a pink verbena at bottom left foreground.*

A VERSATILE WINDOWBOX

Windowboxes are on show all the time and so the whole display can be spoiled if one plant is past its best. In this case, it pays to leave plants in their pots and just 'plunge' them into the container up to their rims. You can then lift out and replace individual plants without disturbing the others, leaving a wreath of foliage such as trailing ivy round the edge and altering the flowers in between them as the seasons change. You might choose spring bulbs and polyanthus for instant color in spring, replacing them with annuals, pelargoniums or fuchsias, or perhaps a mixture of culinary and flowering herbs for the summer.

In the fall and winter, big cities create their own mild microclimate, allowing you to plant cool-temperature indoor plants, such as cyclamen and exacum, in windowboxes out of doors. To be on the safe side, do not try this unless you have seen other people in your area use the strategy successfully.

2 Arrange the plants in front of the windowbox. Place 1 inch of soilless potting mix in the liner and make a small depression for each pot to stand in.

This Swan River daisy will form the central part of the arrangement.

1 This wooden windowbox has its own rigid plastic liner. It prevents the wood being in contact with damp soil, which could cause the wood to rot. There are no drainage holes.

3 Place the plants, in their pots, into the box. In this formal, symmetrical display, trails of ivy cascade over the sides and flowering plants are grouped together in the center.

A VERSATILE WINDOWBOX

When planting up a windowbox, it is worth leaving foliage plants in their pots, too, so that they can be easily replaced if necessary. As well as ivies, small upright conifer trees and many houseplants (such as asparagus fern) can be used as temporary foliage plants for windowboxes. To look after a windowbox display like this, feed and water the plants regularly. Check the potting mix daily in summer and in windy weather, when they are liable to dry out more rapidly. And keep the soil around the pots moist; as well as helping to keep the plants watered, this creates a humid pocket of air around the plants, which they enjoy

4 Fill the space between the pots with more potting mix. This helps to keep the pots in place and retains moisture, acting as a reserve from which the plants can draw as needed.

5 It is easy to lift out fading plants and replace them with fresh ones. Experiment with new 'looks' or alter the composition for a change.

Swan River daisy (Brachycome)

Pelargonium

Ageratum

Trailing ivy

Ringing the changes

Here, just the *Brachycome* and two of the ageratums have been lifted out of the middle of the display and replaced with a tuberous-rooted begonia. This clearly shows the effect that even a small change can make on the arrangement.

1 Select a suitable container with several holes in the base. This one is actually made from styrofoam. Place 1 inch of gravel in the bottom to improve the drainage.

2 Put the largest rock in place before filling the container with potting mix. This makes it easier to move.

3 Fill the container almost to the rim with soil-based potting mixture; this can be mixed with a small amount of fine grit to improve drainage even more.

A ROCKERY IN A TROUGH

Few gardens today have room for a conventional rockery, but a miniature version in a container makes a most attractive feature on paving near a back door or seat. Team rockery-themed containers with gravel or cobbled paths or tuck them into odd sunny corners around the garden. Stone sinks were once the traditional containers for alpines, but you can use virtually any container, as long as it can withstand frost and has good drainage. Large terracotta pots, deep ceramic dishes and plastic troughs are all suitable. Check that there are plenty of holes in the base; if not, drill more. The larger the container, the easier it is to have something in flower all the time as you can get more plants into it.

4 Add a couple of smaller rocks to complement the larger chunk. Again, partly bury them in the potting mixture for a more natural effect and to prevent them becoming dislodged.

5 Choose a selection of rock plants with different shapes, flower colors and leaf textures. Stand the pots roughly in position while you plan where to plant each one.

A ROCKERY IN A TROUGH

Nurseries and garden centers offer a huge range of rockery plants, but vigorous spreading kinds will soon become a nuisance in a confined space, so restrict yourself to compact cushion- and bun-shaped plants. If you choose spreading plants such as aubretia, which make carpets of color, place them at the edge of the container so they can trail over the sides and make sure you can replace them easily with smaller plants when they outgrow their welcome. Since the majority of popular rock plants are spring-flowering, include plants with attractive, preferably evergreen, foliage to keep the display looking good all year round. You can also find ultra-dwarf trees, such as *Betula nana*, to help create mini-landscapes in planted troughs.

6 Knock each plant out of its pot, and scoop out a hole in the potting mix large enough to take the roots comfortably. Avoid breaking up the rootball of the plant.

7 Topdress with a layer of fine grit, which helps prevent the necks of the plants rotting. Grit and stone chippings are available in a range of suitable colors.

8 To keep the rockery looking its best, trim back dead stems and sprinkle fresh gravel around the plants in spring, feed and water it in summer and protect it from excess rain in winter by raising it up on bricks to allow surplus water to drain away.

Saxifraga cotyledon 'Southside Seedling'

Arenaria balearica

Primula auricula

Saxifraga 'Cloth of Gold'

Aubretia 'Blue Down'

Saxifraga 'Fleece'

Oxalis adenophylla

Viola 'Molly Sanderson'

Silene 'Druett's Variegated'

Saxifraga 'Silver Cushion'

Arabis fernandii-coburgii 'Variegata'

Saxifraga 'Peter Pan'

Sempervivum 'Commander Hay'

CLEMATIS IN A WOODEN TROUGH

Thin strips of wood, pulled across and interlocked under tension, form the support.

Few gardeners realize the value of clematis as a container-grown plant for the patio. Here we have used a wooden trough with an integral support, but you can use any suitable container and support system. You can grow a clematis like this in most locations and even move it when decoration or repairs are necessary. Wooden containers tend to weather with age and eventually rot unless you protect them. The most effective and safest way is to paint them with an acrylic-based product, available in a wide range of colors and harmless to plants. Brush hardwood containers with a little teak oil from time to time to keep them fresh. Depending on the size of container, you can plant more than one clematis in it or fill the base with other plants. The best choices are the large-flowered mid-season varieties with their stunning blooms, the smaller species, such as *C. alpina* and *C. florida*, and some of the more tender, early flowering types, such as *C. forsteri* and *C. armandii*.

Loosely secure the shoots, using paper-covered wire plant ties.

Water the trough well in at this stage and continue to do so throughout the summer.

1 Place your container in position. Put in a layer of crocks or stones to improve the drainage and fill it with a good-quality, well-balanced potting mixture. Do not use garden soil.

2 Gently lower the clematis into place, with a few buds below the surface, and firm it well in. Make sure that there are no air gaps around the roots to prevent the plant from establishing itself.

3 In this trough, we have used hostas to fill the space around the base of the plant. They make a fine contrast with the clematis and grow well in shade, but do require plenty of water to succeed.

4 After a few weeks, begin feeding the plants with tomato fertilizer to ensure that the clematis gives a good display of flowers all summer.

CLEMATIS IN A LARGE PATIO CONTAINER

This sort of container and its supports were designed primarily for growing runner beans, but it also works well with clematis. Because of its width, it holds adequate potting mixture, not only for the clematis, but also for a few bedding plants at the base. Here we have used *Begonia semperflorens*, but you could plant any low-growing annual. Alternatively, some of the Mediterranean plants with silver leaves will also thrive at the base of a clematis. Try one of the artemisias, such as *Artemisia frigida*, perhaps with some spring crocus underplanted to start the display. When selecting the clematis, use the more compact types, such as 'Lady Northcliffe' and 'Comtesse de Bouchaud', as here. The flowering periods of these two varieties overlap, which extends the period of interest of the container, and they require different pruning strategies. 'Lady Northcliffe' needs a light prune and 'Comtesse de Bouchaud', a hard prune, but the nature of the supports allows you to do this with ease. Remember that the container is open to the weather on all sides and that large-flowered clematis may be damaged by strong summer winds.

1 Choose a potting mixture that will sustain your plants for several years. Clematis grow best in moist, well-drained, fertile soil, and need a cool root run.

2 Gently place the clematis into the container close to the supports. Make sure the rootball is not damaged and that some buds will be below soil level.

3 Once the clematis are secured, fill the remaining space with plants of your choice, ensuring that both they and the clematis are firmed in well.

4 Water the plants in until some water escapes from the base of the container. If the potting mixture is well balanced, overwatering is not a problem.

5 After about two months, your efforts will be rewarded with a superb show of flowers that will continue to give pleasure throughout the summer months.

The flowers should stretch from top to bottom of the supports. These are 'Comtesse de Bouchaud'.

Plants at the base give the container a well-furnished appearance and help to prevent water loss through evaporation.

Clematis 'Lady Northcliffe' is a compact variety that blooms all summer.

These begonias are ideal companion plants.

75

ALPINES IN HYPERTUFA

Any plants that will grow in normal containers will also grow in hypertufa, but stone or hypertufa containers are mostly used for rock plants. All sorts of alpines, dwarf bulbs and drought-tolerant small shrubs are suitable, as long as you only group together plants that share similar soil conditions and cultural requirements. Plants that need particularly well-drained potting mix, such as encrusted saxifrages, armerias, erodiums, sedums, sempervivums and lewisias, do best in a mixture of 1 part grit to 4 parts soil-based potting mix. Less fussy rock plants, such as arabis, aubretia, diascia and most campanulas are quite happy in soil-based potting mix on its own. Larger shrubby rock plants for stone or fake stone containers include helianthemum, cistus and hebes: the whipcord hebes have dramatic stringlike foliage, although others have more striking flowers.

2 Whatever soil you use, put a 1-2-inch layer of coarse gravel over the base to assist drainage and stop crocks becoming clogged.

3 For growing alpines in this container, add 1 part of coarse grit to 4 parts of soil-based potting mixture.

Fill the container almost to the rim.

Coarse grit

Soil-based potting mix

1 Cover the drainage holes in the base of the container with crocks to stop the soil trickling out. Surplus water can still escape.

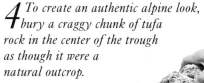

4 To create an authentic alpine look, bury a craggy chunk of tufa rock in the center of the trough as though it were a natural outcrop.

5 A hole left by an air pocket in the hypertufa mixture makes a planting pocket for a sedum, pushed through from outside.

ALPINES IN HYPERTUFA

Other suitable plants for alpine containers include small hardy cranesbills, such as *Geranium lancastriense*, and gentians, but give gentians relatively moisture-retentive soil as they dislike drying out; a half-and-half mixture of peat- and soil-based potting soils with a little added grit would be best. (Do check plant care labels with gentians as some varieties only grow in lime-free soil.) They also like partial shade. In a very shady spot, fill the container with the peat/soil mix and plant ramonda and haberlea or primula species and small hardy ferns, such as *Adiantum pedatum*, the bird's foot fern, and *Adiantum venustum*, the hardy maidenhair fern. They all need rather damper conditions than normal alpines; the soil should never quite dry out.

6 *Choose a selection of alpines that need the same soil and growing conditions. Flowering kinds and those with hillocky shapes and colored foliage make interesting combinations.*

7 *Evergreen plants look interesting in winter when many alpines die down to ground level. In time, they will creep over the sides of the trough and up the tufa chunk.*

8 *Topdress the finished surface with coarse grit, such as granite chippings. It improves surface drainage and prevents alpines rotting at the neck.*

Sedum spurium 'Variegatum'

Rhodohypoxis 'Fred Broome'

Sedum 'Lydium'

Campanula muralis

Saxifraga correovensis

Sempervivum *hybrid*

Erodium 'Natasha'

9 *The planted container already begins to look like real stone. You can spray the sides with dilute liquid feed to encourage mosses and lichens to grow.*

Patio pots

Containers are to patios what pot plants are to living rooms; they are the final touches that complete the exterior decorating scheme. This section shows you how use them with flair.

Contents

SPRING ANNUALS - PANSIES

If you grow spring annuals from seed, you could plant containers in late summer or early fall for the following spring. But they need careful attention in winter, and it is easier to leave the plants in trays or small pots in a cold greenhouse and plant them just as they are coming into flower. If you buy in your plants, you will find plenty of spring annuals to choose from. Forget-me-nots, spring bulbs in individual pots and pansies are very popular. As a change from planting up the greatest mixture of flowers that will fit into a large container, try teaming a prettily patterned pot with flowers that pick out one of the colors from the pot. Or stand a row of similar pots in a row along the top of a low wall. Pansies are particularly attractive and are available in a good range of colors, some with delightful 'faces'.

1 *Cover the drainage hole with a crock before packing in as many plants as possible. A small pot like this takes four. Loosely fill with potting mix to within 1 inch of the rim.*

3 *When they are in place, fill the gaps between them with potting mix, leaving about ½ inch between the top of the soil and the rim of the pot for watering.*

2 *Remove each plant by pushing it up through the hole in the base of the compartment. You may need to squeeze the rootballs gently to fit them into the container.*

4 *If any potting mix spills onto the container during planting, wipe it off so that the pot is clean. Stand the pot on its matching saucer.*

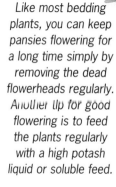

Like most bedding plants, you can keep pansies flowering for a long time simply by removing the dead flowerheads regularly. Another tip for good flowering is to feed the plants regularly with a high potash liquid or soluble feed.

This frost-resistant, ceramic pot is decorated with an oriental-style floral design in purple to echo the pansies.

5 *Water the pansies in. As the pot is packed full of plants, it will dry out quite quickly, so check it regularly and especially during hot weather to see if it needs watering again.*

A PLASTIC TUB OF ANNUALS

Because plastic containers are not porous, the potting mixture in them does not dry out so quickly. This is a benefit on hot summer days, but can be a problem at the start of the season, as small, young plants do not use much water, especially in cool weather, and it is easy to overwater them. Plastic pots usually have several drainage holes, but as these are quite small, there is no need to cover them with crocks. Some people prefer plastic containers for plants that only last one season - typically spring or summer annuals. This is probably a throwback to the days when poor-quality plastic containers were liable to disintegrate in a hard frost. But nowadays, good-quality plastics last much better and can be used outdoors all year round.

1 Group a selection of plants to see how they look together. This is a bright color scheme of red, yellow and orange. One plant is a climber, so put a cane in the middle of the tub to support it.

Choose a soilless potting mixture and fill the tub to just below the rim.

2 Plant the centerpiece first - here a climbing black-eyed Susan. Tie it loosely to the cane and tie in new stems regularly.

3 A foliage plant makes a good 'foil' for groups of flowers. This coleus goes very well with the color scheme of the container.

4 Water the finished container. It should look well filled with plants; as they grow, the effect will become even more abundant-looking. Once the container is filled with roots, water it once or twice a day, especially in hot weather.

Black-eyed Susan (Thunbergia alata)

Argyranthemum frutescens 'Jamaica Primrose'

African marigold, compact type

Ornamental cabbage

French marigold 'Aurora Fire'

Salvia 'Vanguard'

Coleus

A COTTAGE GARDEN FEATURE FOR THE PATIO

A patio paved with old stone slabs, cobbles and gravel would suit a cottage-style garden. Containers in a good range of sizes and made of natural-looking materials, such as terracotta flowerpots, blend in best. Small pots look good in a row along the edge of garden steps or on top of a low wall – use them to grow drought-resistant sempervivums, sedums or red pelargoniums. Larger pots suit single specimen plants of fuchsia, marguerite or perennial herbs. You could also plant a mixture of colorful cottage garden annuals in big pots; these can stand alone or be grouped together with other plants. Spring bulbs, primroses, violets, wallflowers, pansies and stocks are good for spring color. Plant them in spring, just as they are coming into flower.

1 Choose some old-fashioned annual flowers and a pair of large matching clay flowerpots, one larger than the other.

3 Choose something striking and colorful as the centerpiece of the smaller pot, but allow the centerpiece of the biggest pot to dominate the display.

2 First plant the biggest and boldest plant towards the center back of the larger pot as a focal point. Use slightly shorter flowers to go round it.

4 Finish off with a 'fringe' of low sprawling plants along the front of the arrangement – a row of this type of plant would have been used in an old cottage garden to edge the path.

Snapdragon (Antirrhinum 'Coronette Scarlet')

Mixed snapdragons

Nicotiana 'Lime Green'

Dwarf sunflower

Argyranthemum foeniculaceum

White alyssum

5 The two pots blend together to become part of the same display. Feed, water and deadhead regularly.

Pelargonium 'Ringo Scarlet'

1 Select enough drought-resistant, non-hardy flowers and herbs to slightly overfill a terracotta pot. Plant into any good-quality, peat- or soil-based potting mix.

2 Knock each plant gently out of its pot. Carefully tease out any large roots without breaking up the rootball.

3 Place taller, upright plants, such as this bay tree, in the middle of the pot, with lower and trailing plants around the edge.

A MEDITERRANEAN DISPLAY

Patios originated in the Mediterranean region, where the hot dry climate makes it more practical to have an enclosed yard with paved floor and drought-tolerant plants growing in containers made of local materials. There would also be a vine growing over pergola poles for shade. Today, anyone can create a Mediterranean-style patio at home. White walls, simple garden furniture, a vine - perhaps an ornamental one, such as the purple-leaved *Vitis vinifera* 'Purpurea' - and colorful pots of flowers are the basic ingredients. Red pelargoniums are a Mediterranean favorite, but more sophisticated flowers are just as suitable. Daisy shapes are a good choice - choose blue kingfisher daisy (*Felicia amelloides*), osteospermum or Swan River daisy (*Brachycome*). Succulent plants with thick fleshy leaves look at home here, too. Look for Livingstone daisy (*Mesembryanthemum criniflorum*), lampranthus and portulaca for flowers. Pots of ordinary cacti and succulents can stand outside for the summer. Perennial herbs, such as bay and rosemary, can be grown as specimen plants; pots of bush basil near a patio door are said to keep flies from going indoors. Larger, shrubby Mediterranean-style plants, such as bottlebrush, and potted climbers, such as bougainvillea, can also stand outside on the patio in summer, but as they are not hardy in cool temperate climates, move them to a frost-free greenhouse or sunroom for the winter. Grow annual climbers up walls and trellis - morning glory (*Ipomoea purpurea*) is a very typically Mediterranean plant.

4 Distribute colorful flowers evenly throughout the display. Tuck in small but dense patches of color to balance up the display's visual impact.

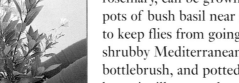

Osteospermum 'Silver Sparkler'

Bay (Laurus nobilis)

Osteospermum 'Pink Whirls'

Basil 'Dark Opal'

Helichrysum microphylla

Cockscomb (Celosia cristata)

A SCENTED POT TO BRING FRAGRANCE TO THE PATIO

1 *Half fill the pot with soil. Make sure that there is room for the plants to stand on top of the soil leaving a 1-inch gap between the top of the rootballs and the rim of the pot.*

Plant fragrances linger longest in warm, still air, so a patio is the ideal place to enjoy them. Perfumed plants fall into two groups; those with scented leaves and those with fragrant flowers. Of the two, those with scented leaves are most valuable in containers, as the effect lasts longer. To release the scent from leaves you must bruise them very slightly, so place the container next to a door where you will brush past the plants or near a seat where you can touch the leaves. Herbs and scented-leaved pelargoniums are the best subjects, as they are reliably fragrant, yet compact enough for pots. Lemon verbena (*Lippia citriodora*), lavender, eau de cologne mint (*Mentha citrata*), pineapple sage (*Salvia rutilans*) and rose geranium (*Pelargonium graveolens*) are the best known. There are also various spicily scented plants, such as *Nepeta citriodora* (lemon scented leaves). Bear in mind that apart from a few exceptions, most plants with scented leaves are not as striking or colorful as the majority of bedding plants, so do not expect a dazzling display.

2 *Select three scented plants that go well together, and gently tap them out of their pots. Place the first one close to the edge of the pot, turning it so that any overhanging shoots cascade over the side.*

Basil mint

Lavender 'Hidcote'

Scented-leaved pelargonium 'Lady Plymouth'

4 *Put the finished display in a sunny, sheltered spot on the patio, where the scent will linger longest. Avoid overwatering for maximum perfume-power, but do not let the plants wilt.*

3 *Add the final plant. Choose contrasting leaf shapes, size and texture - include a variegated plant and one that has pretty flowers, as well as scented foliage.*

Place the tallest plant at the back of the container.

1 Put a crock over the drainage hole and about 1 inch of gravel over the crock to prevent soil washing out when you water. It also provides the sharp drainage rock plants need.

2 Almost fill the container with soil. Add some potting grit and mix the two together. 1 part grit to 6 of potting mix is fine for the rock plants in this display.

A POTTED ROCK GARDEN

Rock plants are becoming very popular subjects for containers, with good reason. The plants are small but distinctive, and since few people can spare the space or the time to look after a full-sized rock garden, a potted one is the practical way to enjoy these charming plants. Rock plants naturally associate well together, but be sure to choose plants that share similar growing requirements. Most need a sunny spot and reasonably good drainage, so raise the container up on two bricks so that it does not stand in a puddle of water. Choose plants with different shapes, colors, textures and flower types for the best display. Foliage plants make a long-term background for seasonal flowers. For flowers, choose a mixture of plants whose flowering times overlap to keep the container colorful from spring to late summer.

3 Sink a craggy chunk of rock into the middle of the pot for a realistic background. This is tufa, a type of porous limestone.

4 Choose a mixture of plants with long flowering seasons, plus some good foliage kinds. Arrange them around the pot and begin planting. Start by putting in the biggest plants.

5 Tuck trailing plants in round the edge to soften the sharp outlines. Finish off by troweling decorative gravel between the plants. It looks good and holds the plants up off the potting mix.

Campanula carpatica

Diascia 'Ruby Field'

Tanacetum densum 'Amani'

Dianthus 'Whatfield Ruby'

6 Water the plants well, allow the soil to dry out just a little and water again. Scrape away some gravel to feel the soil.

Pratia pedunculata

Festuca glacialis

GRASSES IN TERRACOTTA

A large container filled with a mixture of contrasting grasses looks particularly striking in a modern setting, where the dramatic shapes really stand out well. Team it with smaller containers of evergreens, conifers and heathers to make a fuller display. Ornamental grasses range in height from several inches up to several feet. The tall bamboos *Arundo donax* and *Miscanthus* are best grown in large tubs of their own once they have reached a good size. A row of these makes a good instant screen. But while they are young, they could be used for a year or two in large mixed plantings with other species. Medium-sized grasses include Bowles golden grass (*Milium effusum* 'Aureum'), *Carex comans* (an unusual bronze form of sedge which, although not a true grass, does looks like one), *Hakonechloa macra* 'Albo-aurea' (a graceful, striped grass with gold and green leaves) and *Helictotrichon sempervirens*, which has wide, ribbonlike, steel-blue foliage. Among the smaller grasses are many species of festuca, which have vivid blue foliage.

1 Cover the drainage holes with a crock and half fill the pot with good-quality potting mix. Knock the plants out of their pots, carefully placing each one right up against the side of the pot. Start with the largest plant.

2 Tuck the next plant in alongside the first, pushing it well up to leave room for the third. Although space is a bit tight, fill the container well for a display that looks instantly mature.

Bowles golden grass (Milium effusum 'Aureum')

Miscanthus sinensis 'Zebrinus'

Carex comans

3 Fit in the last plant, squeezing the rootballs if necessary. Arrange trailing leaves so that they hang freely over the edge of the pot.

4 After watering in, move the container to its final position. Put it with potted specimen shrubs, particularly evergreens, or stand it on gravel, say in an oriental-style area of the garden.

HYDRANGEAS - IDEAL FOR A SHADY PATIO

If the only place available for a patio is in shade, you can still grow some very fine plants. One of the very best flowering container shrubs for shade is hydrangea. Choose any of the mophead or lacecap varieties and a large pot - at least 15 inches in diameter. Plant blue varieties in ericaceous soil, but use normal potting mixture for varieties that are supposed to be pink. Keep hydrangeas exceptionally well fed and watered, as they are gluttons. After flowering, it is normal to leave the dead flower heads on to protect the young shoots from winter weather. Late the following spring, cut these stems back to where the first young shoot grows out of them. Other good plants for shade include a huge range of ivies, *Ajuga*, hardy ferns and hostas. Box does well in shade as long as it gets two hours of sun each day, and the plain green Mexican orange (*Choisya ternata*) is happy in shade and has white flowers in early summer. Camellias and dwarf rhododendrons are also good pot subjects, given ericaceous mix, and dappled rather than deep shade.

Pink hydrangeas can be grown in normal potting mix.

1 The container should be at least 2-3 inches larger in both diameter and depth than the pot in which the plant is growing when you acquire it.

2 Plant the shrub into a soil-based potting mix and fill in the gap between the rootball and the pot. Sprinkle a little fresh soil over the top of the rootball to cover any exposed roots and protect them from drying out. Or use some bark chippings as a mulch.

3 Water the plant well in so that the soil is thoroughly moist. Check the plant daily in summer and water it so that the soil is always very moist.

4 The planted container makes a good specimen pot placed out of direct sun or in full shade. Feed regularly. Do not deadhead hydrangeas until early spring.

A POT FOR A SHADY PLACE

Shady areas can difficult to 'decorate' with pots, but many plants that are suitable for shady gardens grow well in containers. Hydrangeas and hostas make good specimen plants on their own in large pots, but group small plants together in large containers. All the plants featured here are moisture-lovers, so select a moisture-retaining container. Good plants include lady's mantle (*Alchemilla mollis*), *Ajuga* (ornamental bugle, which has colored leaves and blue flowers), cultivated celandines, *Pulmonaria* (lungwort), which has silver spotted leaves, *Brunnera* (perennial forget-me-not), plus camellia and miniature rhododendrons. Few annuals will tolerate shade for more than half a day, but *Impatiens* will thrive if they are already flowering when you plant them.

3 *Plant the foliage plant first – here a hardy fern – and add the flowering plants next. Knock each one carefully out of its pot and plant it without breaking up the rootball.*

4 *Finish off by tucking a few trailing plants, such as the ivies used here, around the sides to soften the edge of the container.*

1 *Fill the pot to within 2 inches of its rim with soil–based potting mixture. This will suit the perennials to be planted here, as they will remain in the container for several years and its weight keeps the pot stable.*

2 *Leaving them in their pots for the time being, stand the plants in the container while you decide which ones look best together.*

Hardy fern (Dryopteris filix-mas 'Crispula Crispata')

Drumstick primula (Primula denticulata)

Primrose (Primula vulgaris)

Ivy (Hedera helix)

Viola labradorica

5 *To finish off, twist the ivy trails to form a definite edge to the planting, instead of letting them dangle over the sides. Hold the ends in place with paper-covered wire ties.*

CREATING A BONSAI CONIFER

Good plants for an oriental-style garden include almond, peach, rhododendron and azalea, ornamental quince *(Chaenomeles)*, flowering cherry, bamboo and Japanese maple *(Acer palmatum* cultivars). You can trim evergreens and conifers into approximations of bonsai shapes, even when they are growing in the ground. Another effective way of trimming them is to leave bare stems at the base of the plant and clip the foliage to resemble 'clouds' at the top. Good conifers for clipping include the blue-leaved *Chamaecyparis pisifera* 'Boulevard' and dwarf cultivars of *C. lawsoniana*, such as 'Green Globe'. Trees and shrubs that grow naturally into dramatic bonsai-like shapes include the dwarf Mount Fuji cherry *(Prunus incisa* 'Kojo no Mai'), twiggy, upright *Prunus* 'Amanogawa', contorted hazel, and unusual weeping conifers, such as *Sequoiadendron giganteum* 'Pendulum'. Poorly shaped specimens of azalea and other oriental-look shrubs can be a cheap buy in garden centers and are easily pruned into lopsided 'bonsai' shapes.

Real bonsai trees are best left to enthusiasts as they require special care, but you can achieve a similar effect by growing traditional bonsai subjects in much larger pots and trimming them into freehand oriental shapes, just for fun.

1 Trim away the lower leaves of the conifer to accentuate the trunklike appearance of the lower stem, removing all dead leaves and bare shoots.

After removing brown leaves, all the growth left should be fresh and healthy.

2 Spread out the main branches to see the basic structure and decide how to use it.

3 Thin out some of the growth from the base of the plant to expose the outline of the main branches growing out from the 'trunk'. The aim is to create a plant with a craggy, aged look.

4 As you thin out the plant, aim for an asymmetrical shape that looks as if it has been naturally sculpted by the wind. Shorten some shoots to leave stubs along the branches, for character.

Chamaecyparis pisifera 'Boulevard'

Rubbing the scales off the stems gives them a smoother finish.

5 Stop when you think you have done enough. The finished tree should have a good basic framework of exposed branches with a well-balanced spread of foliage towards the tips.

HEBE AND GINKGO IN ORIENTAL STYLE

Some conifers and evergreens naturally grow into striking shapes without much clipping and trimming. Alternatively, you could group a collection of choice, truly dwarf conifers and evergreens on a patio in matching weatherproof pots. For compact, globular shapes, go for *Chamaecyparis* 'Gnome' and *Hebe* 'Green Globe'; for a compact craggy spire choose *Chamaecyparis obtusa* 'Tetragona Aurea', or for shaggy curls go for *Pinus mugo* 'Pumilio'. Since these are not being treated as true bonsai trees, choose pots of a suitable size for each plant and a soil-based potting mix. After a year or two, move the plants to a pot one size larger in spring. When a plant reaches the maximum desired size, repot it back into the same pot after trimming away about one quarter of the fine roots from the edge of the rootball.

Acer palmatum 'Atropurpureum'

Maidenhair tree (Ginkgo biloba)

Hebe 'Green Globe'

1 Ginkgo biloba, *the maiden-hair tree, is a good choice for clipping into an oriental-inspired shape. Bend the horizontal shoots over and tie them in place to accentuate the effect.*

2 *Pull down the two shoots so that they lie roughly parallel, with one echoing the curve of the other. The shape should have 'set' within a year, and then you can remove the string.*

3 *Before completing potting, experiment by tipping the tree to see if you can create a better 'bonsai shape' by inclining the stem at an angle. An irregular shape often looks best.*

Trimming a hebe

Starting at the top, snip back growth to establish a natural outline. Side shoots will appear from below the cut ends, making a bushier shape. Trim once a year after the main flush of growth.

PLANTING BULBS IN A CONTAINER

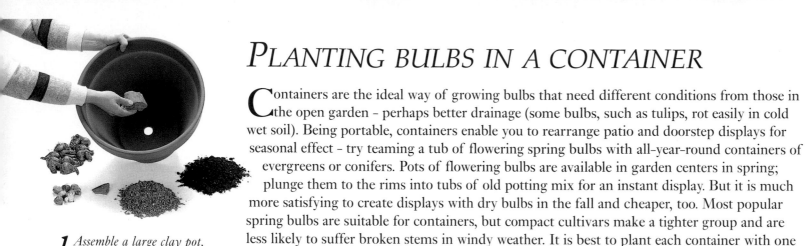

Containers are the ideal way of growing bulbs that need different conditions from those in the open garden - perhaps better drainage (some bulbs, such as tulips, rot easily in cold wet soil). Being portable, containers enable you to rearrange patio and doorstep displays for seasonal effect - try teaming a tub of flowering spring bulbs with all-year-round containers of evergreens or conifers. Pots of flowering bulbs are available in garden centers in spring; plunge them to the rims into tubs of old potting mix for an instant display. But it is much more satisfying to create displays with dry bulbs in the fall and cheaper, too. Most popular spring bulbs are suitable for containers, but compact cultivars make a tighter group and are less likely to suffer broken stems in windy weather. It is best to plant each container with one type of bulb, but if you mix different kinds together, choose those that flower at the same time, otherwise the display will be spoiled by old foliage when the later ones come into bloom. Start liquid feeding regularly when the first buds appear.

6 Trowel more potting mix carefully over the grape hyacinth bulbs. Fill the pot to within 1in of the rim. Leave some space for watering.

'Pot feet' improve drainage.

1 Assemble a large clay pot, gritty sand, soil-based potting mixture and your chosen bulbs. Cover the hole in the base of the pot with a broken 'crock'.

A soil-based potting mixture is best for bulbs, as it retains less water than peat types.

Bulbs are best in clay pots, as these are porous.

2 Scoop 1-2 inches of gritty sand into the base of the pot over the crock. Add 1-2 inches of potting mixture, so that the pot is roughly half-filled. Do not firm down the mixture at this stage.

3 Press the bulbs gently into the potting mix. Put in as many as you can for a good display. Adjacent bulbs should not quite touch each other or the side of the pot. These are daffodils.

4 Carefully cover the daffodil bulbs with more potting mixture, leaving only the tips showing. This allows a second tier of bulbs to be planted in the gaps without risk of damage.

5 Grape hyacinths flower at the same time as daffodils and have similar requirements, but plant them less deeply. Press the bulbs between the daffodils.

A HONEYSUCKLE IN A TUB

Honeysuckles are universal favorites and there are many different species and cultivars to choose from. They can be grown in hedgerows, up trees, as pillars or as specimens in a tub with a support. They are energetic stem climbers, have spectacular flowers and can fill the evening air with evocative scents. So which do you choose? There is a good chance that your native honeysuckle will perform the best in your area, but there are many others, such as *Lonicera periclymenum* or *L. etrusca*, that you can grow as species of honeysuckles. Other good performers include *Lonicera* x *americana*, 'Gold Flame' and the favorite, 'Graham Thomas' featured here. You might also consider Japanese honeysuckle, *L. japonica* 'Aureoreticulata' or the yellow trumpet honeysuckle, *L. sempervirens f. sulphurea*. In areas that enjoy a typical Mediterranean climate, the Burmese honeysuckle, *Lonicera hildebrandtiana*, can look staggering with its 7-inch-long yellow-orange giant flowers. This powerful climber is ideal for growing on pergolas, where it will relish the sunny conditions.

1 Fill the tub with a suitable potting mixture and make a hole in the center large enough for the rootball to fit with ease, allowing about 2 inches of potting mixture below the roots.

2 Tap the nursery plant out of its pot, together with its cane, and place the rootball into the hole, taking care not to lose too much of the soil adhering to the roots. Firm it in well.

3 Gently firm in the soil around the plant to eliminate air gaps, which would prevent the roots developing. Add more potting mix if necessary, but leave a space at the top for watering.

4 Use soft string to tie the cane to the trellis and to tie in individual climbing stems. Tie the knots loosely to avoid stem damage.

5 Give the honeysuckle a generous watering to ensure that it gets off to a good start. Water it every day for ten days so that it becomes established and do not allow it to dry out after that.

A CLASSIC STRAWBERRY POT

Strawberries are both ornamental and productive in containers. If you do not have room for a conventional strawberry bed, a planter such as this is ideal, as you can pack plenty of plants into a very small space. For early strawberries, move the planter into a cold or slightly heated greenhouse in midwinter and the fruit will be ready to pick several weeks earlier than usual. Strawberry plants can be bought cheaply as young 'runners' in the fall or as pot-grown plants in the fall and spring. Continue planting even when the plants are in flower, but do not allow the roots to dry out. Most strawberries look pretty when flowering, but now you can obtain varieties with pink flowers instead of white ones. Some of these are intended to be mainly ornamental, with small fruits as a bonus, but others also produce a good crop. Water them well and feed every week with liquid tomato feed, from flowering time until after the crop has been picked.

3 As you complete each layer of plants, top the container up with more potting mixture to just below the base of the next row of planting pockets until you reach the rim of the pot.

4 Depending on the size of the container, plant two or three strawberry plants in the top of the pot so that it is well filled. Use a little more potting mixture to fill any gaps between the plants.

'Serenata' has pink flowers and a useful crop of fruit.

2 Knock the plants out of their pots. The rootballs of pot-grown strawberries will be too big to fit into the planting pockets, so plant them from the inside. Firm the potting mix around the roots.

Hold the rootball under the planting pocket and gently push the leafy top of the plant out through the hole.

1 Cover the large drainage hole in the base of this pot with a small handful of crocks. Fill the pot to 1 inch below the bottom row of planting pockets in the side, using a soil-based potting mixture.

5 Stand the pot in a sheltered, sunny spot. Feed and water it regularly. Replace the potting mix and the plants every two or three years for good crops.

WINTER-FLOWERING TUBS

All the plants suggested for winter hanging baskets are equally suitable for containers. Being closer to ground level, tubs suffer less from the weather, so you can grow a wider range of plants, including winter-flowering heathers, Christmas rose *(Helleborus niger)*, early spring bulbs and early spring bedding plants. Use taller plants, such as evergreen shrubs, as the centerpiece of a floral display; variegated or colored kinds, such as euonymus and *Choisya ternata* 'Sundance', whipcord *Hebe* 'James Stirling' or dwarf conifers, are good. Plants bought straight from a garden center are ideal. Shrubs can remain in their new tubs for a couple of years, but will fairly quickly fill them with root, preventing new bedding plants being put in to replace those that are over. So unless the plant is to become a solo specimen, repot it with new flowers into a larger container each fall, or plant it out into the garden in spring.

1 Assemble a large container, potting mix and a variety of plants, including an evergreen shrub, trailing ivies and winter-flowering annuals.

2 Start by putting the largest plant in the center of the tub. Keep the rootball intact, as space will be short and there are several other plants to put in.

3 A large plant, such as ivy, trailing over the tub softens the straight edges and helps the evergreen to blend in with the arrangement.

4 Fit in as many flowering plants as possible. Once in bloom, they do not grow any more, so the finished result must provide the full impact.

Winter-flowering evergreens, such as Skimmia japonica 'Rubella', look good in containers.

Cultivated primrose hybrids (Primula acaulis hybrids)

5 Pull out strands of ivy for a wispy effect. Sit the arrangement in a prominent position. Water in well. Apply a weak feed during mild spells.

Variegated ivy

93

Wall baskets

Where space is limited, wall baskets and planters provide the ideal form of 'vertical gardening'. Try them and you will be amazed at the range of plants you can grow.

Contents

PLANTING UP A PLASTIC WALL PLANTER

Some wall planters have a wire framework that needs lining in much the same way as a traditional hanging basket. However, unless you have plenty of time for watering, open-sided wall planters can be rather disappointing, as the plants in them dry out almost in front of your eyes. Wall planters with solid sides are generally more practical, but even they dry out quite quickly compared to containers at ground level. This is partly because the containers themselves are so much smaller and also because, being raised up, they are surrounded by breezes that cause water to evaporate from the soil faster than usual. Once you have taken these factors into account, wall planters can look most attractive. Being small, they are usually placed in a 'key' position where they are very visible, so be sure to use only the very best plants in them. Formal arrangements are probably the most suitable, but you could experiment with informal ones. These usually work best if you group a collection of planters in the same style at different levels on a wall. You will only need a very few plants, as the wall planter is only half the width of normal containers.

4 The front row consists of four French marigolds placed in pairs on either side of the coleus. Choose the best plants and use up the rest in other containers or around the garden.

5 The finished display is likely to dry out quickly, so check it twice daily and water it as often as necessary to keep the soil moist and the plants in good condition.

1 If possible, stand the planter on its base while you are planting it. Some do not have a flat base and most are top heavy, so if this is difficult, hang it in its final position and fill it almost to the rim with potting mix.

2 Formal plantings suit these containers well. Here, the centerpiece is a rather striking coleus. You may need to look through a batch of plants before finding a well-shaped specimen.

3 The back row is made up of bedding salvias. From a box of 15 plants, four of the same shape and size were chosen to maintain the symmetrical shape of the design.

Salvia 'Vanguard'

French marigold 'Aurora Fire'

Coleus hybrid

Fill in the spaces between the rootballs with more soil.

A VIVID WALL BASKET

Wall baskets are like hanging baskets that have been sliced in half and mounted on a wall. They are useful where there is not enough room for normal hanging baskets, or where a container mounted flush against the wall looks better. They can add interest to a fence or the side of a shed, and you can hang them from trellis with hooks, or mount them more permanently on a wall. A single wall basket can look rather lonely on a large wall, so group several together for a better display. Threes or fives always look better than even numbers, and a staggered row looks better than a straight line. A single wall basket tends to look best on a short piece of wall, or filling a gap between climbers.

Wall baskets need more watering than normal hanging baskets and frequent feeding. The key to success is matching the plants to the location. For walls in shade for much of the day, choose plants such as mimulus, *Impatiens*, ivies, fuchsias, campanulas and *Begonia semperflorens*. In a hot sunny spot, try lampranthus, echeveria, portulaca and other succulent plants that are naturally drought-proof. Herbs look particularly good in terracotta containers. But for a position that gets sun for about half the day, the usual range of summer-flowering annuals are ideal.

2 This display is based on a pink and mauve scheme. Place the darkest colors in the middle, with the lighter plants towards the outside.

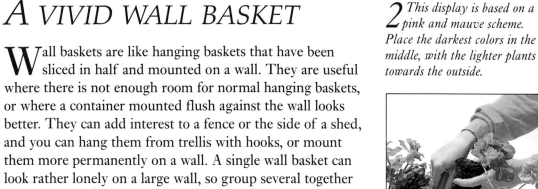

3 Knock the plants out of their pots and plant the rootballs as closely together as possible. The more plants you can pack in, the better the basket will look. Put plants of different colors next to each other.

1 Make sure that there are drainage holes in the base of the basket. Half fill it with a peat-based potting mix that will retain moisture in such a small, densely planted container. Set out your plants.

4 Water the finished basket very well after planting. Expect the soil to dry out very quickly, so check it twice daily. Wall planters can dry out even faster than hanging baskets.

Petunia 'Purple Pirouette'

Ivy-leaved pelargonium 'Summer Showers'

Impatiens 'Accent Lilac'

Ivy-leaved pelargonium 'Butterfly'

HYACINTHS AND PRIMULAS

This scheme is a rich blend of jewel-colored primulas, red hyacinths and warm terracotta shades, more often associated with late summer. The *Primula* 'Wanda' hybrids have introduced a whole set of colors for the spring garden - glowing purples, reds and blues, often further enhanced by dark foliage. Mixed trays of plants may contain white, yellow and pink-flowered forms, so if you want to copy this scheme, wait until one or two buds have opened to check the color or buy plants separately in flower. Heavily scented hyacinths can often be bought in bud as single bulbs and add a luxurious touch to plantings of this kind. Like the hybrid primroses, hyacinths now come in many different colors, including orange and creamy yellow, though as potted bulbs, pinks, blues and white still predominate. The advantage of buying plants in single colors is that color scheming in mixed arrangements is so much easier.

4 *Place the hyacinths against the back of the basket, leaving space for the primulas in front. You may need to shake some of the potting mixture from around the roots to create more room.*

5 *Do not worry if the hyacinths look a little awkward at first; the primroses will soon cover up the base of the bulbs. Lay the plants out first, so that you can work out which color combinations will look the best.*

Reddish pink hyacinths

6 *Winter and spring baskets tend not to grow like summer ones, so cram them full for maximum impact. The primroses will flower for several weeks if well cared for, but hyacinths are not as long-lived. Once their flowers have faded, cut off the heads, but keep the leaves intact.*

Primula 'Wanda' hybrid

Terracotta wall basket with classical-style relief.

1 *Line a terracotta wall basket with black plastic to prevent evaporation through the sides. Cut a hole in the plastic liner to correspond with the drainage hole.*

2 *Add a shallow layer of gravel to provide good drainage. If the basket is left unlined, put a flat stone over the hole to prevent soil loss.*

3 *Cover the gravel with potting mix. Always use fresh potting mix and never garden compost or soil, which contains too many pests and diseases.*

A CHIC TERRACOTTA WALL DISPLAY

1 This container has a rounded base and will not stand upright, so fix it to the wall first. Fill it almost to the brim with soilless potting mixture.

Plain, neutral-colored, classic-style containers are probably the best value plant holders. You can bring them out year after year, planted up with a different set of plants to create a completely new look each time. This terracotta wall planter, for instance, can be planted in several ways. You could choose a traditional plant arrangement, using bedding plants such as tuberous begonias and lobelia as here, or a Mediterranean design based on pelargoniums – the trailing ivy-leaved sort are specially suitable for a wall planter like this. You could use herbs for a scented mixture or try a half-hardy trailing perennial; a single plant is enough to fill a container of this size on its own. Experiment with daring color schemes and bold plant shapes. You can never really tell how plants will look until you see them together, so buy enough for several containers and try out all the possible combinations before deciding which ones to plant together. Pack the container really full of plants and you can easily come up with something quite sensational.

Non-stop begonia 'Rose'

Trailing lobelia 'Crystal Palace'

2 Plant the centerpiece – here a tuberous begonia – first, in the middle of the container, taking care not to damage the rootball.

3 Then add trailing lobelia to fill the rest of the space. The blue of the lobelias will form a vibrant contrast to the deep red of the begonias, and both colors will be set off by the warm tones of the terracotta container.

4 By midsummer you will hardly be able to see the container for the mass of flowers covering it. Be sure to water it often, as this type of porous terracotta container does not hold much soil and dries out quickly.

A FORMAL WALL BASKET

Wall baskets are invariably rather narrow, so a fairly formal, symmetrical arrangement suits them best. A typical formal arrangement is based on a larger 'star' plant in the middle, with smaller supporting plants at the sides. Wire-framed wall baskets are particularly versatile, as you can plant into the sides as well as the top for a fuller display, but we have not done so here in order to keep the rounded shape of the basket. If you do plant the sides and base, use slightly taller plants to balance out the trailing growth below, otherwise the basket will look unbalanced. For maximum effect, 'link' the display in the baskets with other containers or flowerbeds nearby. Or try a display where the same plant or color appears in each basket, even if only in a small way.

1 This traditional style wire-framed wall basket needs lining before planting. There are special liners for 'half' baskets. Alternatively, you could cut a piece of plastic to fit inside.

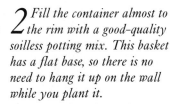

2 Fill the container almost to the rim with a good-quality soilless potting mix. This basket has a flat base, so there is no need to hang it up on the wall while you plant it.

3 The centerpiece of this arrangement is a cascading, or trailing, begonia that will tumble down over the sides of the basket. Deadhead it regularly to keep it flowering all summer.

4 Silver foliage adds sparkle to a display with a lot of similar-looking green leaves. Remove flowers that appear on foliage plants; the leaves deteriorate once flowers develop.

Senecio bicolor (Cineraria maritima)

Floss flower (Ageratum)

5 Water the basket thoroughly and tuck in any flowers or foliage overhanging the back of the basket so they do not get trapped against the wall. Hang the finished container up on the wall.

Cascading begonia 'Finale'

A SIMPLE DECORATIVE WALL PLANTER

Wall planters do not swing in the breeze like a hanging basket, and being flush to the wall offer the plants growing inside rather more warmth and shelter, so use them for your more delicate or heat-loving plants. They are the ideal way to display plants with a naturally floppy habit of growth, such as osteospermums, trailing fuchsias and pendulous begonias, which can spill forward attractively over the edges. Small trailing plants also look very effective. Take advantage of the favored situation to try some of the tougher indoor trailers, such as spider plant *(Chlorophytum)*, wax plant *(Hoya bella)* and creeping fig *(Ficus pumila)* just for the summer. There is no reason why you should not treat the planter like a decorative pot cover and stand a potted plant inside it. This way, it is easy to alter your display every week or two and helps to keep a small garden constantly new and interesting.

2 This is a formal scheme, so tuck in a pair of identical plants on either side to create a pleasing symmetrical display. In this arrangement we have used Helichrysum microphylla.

1 Wall planters do not need many plants to fill them. Part fill the planter with potting mixture and place the largest plant (here an osteospermum) in the middle.

3 Use a little more of the same type of potting mixture to fill the gaps between the rootballs towards the back of the display. Then water thoroughly, and the planter is ready to hang up.

Osteospermum

Helichrysum microphylla

4 Hang the planter on a warm sheltered wall that receives direct sun for at least half the day. Although these plants are fairly drought-tolerant, water them daily in hot weather.

RED PELARGONIUMS IN A BLACK WIRE BASKET

5 *Make sure the plants are far enough inside the basket to avoid drying out. Add the first of the ivy-leaved trailing pelargoniums, arranging the trailing stems so that they point out to the side.*

Romantic, Edwardian-style wirework is back in fashion and you can now buy quite a wide range of elegant designs. Choose plants to match the delicate framework, such as ivy-leaved pelargoniums; their wiry stems covered in attractive foliage create an open, airy effect. Since most baskets are viewed from below, some foliage or flower detail in the sides of the basket is essential. The brightly variegated kingfisher daisy, with its occasional sky blue flowers, is a good choice here, as it enjoys the same conditions as the pelargoniums and never gets too vigorous. Other suitable plants include tender perennials - try the lilac blue-flowered *Brachycome multifida*, a delicate dwarf marguerite, such as *Argyranthemum* 'Petite Pink', and single fuchsias, such as the red-flowered cascade variety 'Marinka'.

1 *Choose sufficient plants to make a good display, leaving some of the basket's intricate decoration visible. Line the back and base of the basket with plastic.*

6 *Fill in any gaps with soil, and water the arrangement thoroughly. Hang it up by hooking the frame over two screws fixed into a sunny wall.*

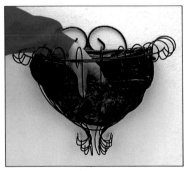

2 *Trim away any excess plastic and then, using thick clumps of moist sphagnum moss, begin lining the front of the basket. Tuck some moss between the wire and the plastic for camouflage.*

3 *Firm down the sphagnum moss so that it forms a solid barrier. Add potting mixture up to the point where you intend to put the first plant in through the front of the wirework basket.*

4 *Guide the shoots of the kingfisher daisies between the wires. Vary the planting heights to avoid straight lines and rest the rootballs horizontally on the soil. Fill around the plants with moss.*

Deadhead flowers as soon as they start to fade.

Variegated Felicia amelloides

A WALL POT OF HERBS

Herbs add significantly to the range of foliage plants that can be used in baskets. For baskets in full sun, try sages, such as the all-purple *Salvia officinalis* 'Purpurascens', the pretty pink, white and purple variegated *S.o.* 'Tricolor' or the yellow-variegated *S.o.* 'Icterina'. Creeping thymes are useful all year round for covering the sides of baskets - plant bushier, more upright types in the top. There are many golden and variegated varieties to choose from; look for them in both the herb and alpine sections of garden centers. For baskets in shade, try using one of the variegated mints, golden marjoram or the feathery-leaved golden feverfew. Herbs make attractive, scented additions to baskets and do well in hot, dry summers, thriving in well-drained conditions and not minding the occasional missed watering.

4 Plant a white trailing or upright verbena in the center and another variegated sage. Deep pink, scarlet, purple or golden-yellow flowers would work as well.

5 Fill in the gaps at each end with more verbenas. Most trailing types will need cutting back now and then, but the blue-purple cascade variety is more delicate.

Salvia officinalis 'Icterina'

Thymus x citriodorus 'Aureus'

Verbena 'Sissinghurst White'

1 Terracotta wall pots in sunny positions lose moisture rapidly, so always line them with plastic before planting. Cut a hole in the liner for drainage matching the hole in the base of the container.

2 Add a layer of gravel or stone chippings. Add a peat-based multipurpose potting mix for a seasonal mixture of herbs and bedding plants. For longer-term plantings, use a soil-based mix.

3 Plant the gold-variegated lemon thyme in the center. Add a variegated sage behind and slightly to one side. The sage will need pinching out to keep it bushy and in scale with the container.

102

A WINTER WALL BASKET

1 Cut a piece of plastic sheeting to line the back of the basket and protect the wall. One corner of an empty potting mixture bag is ideal. Turn the plastic up at the base to form a lip.

The festive looking winter cherry comes into the shops during late fall and makes an ideal subject for a basket by the front door over the holiday period. Here, pure white cyclamen and white-variegated ivy act as a foil for the orange-red berries. For a richer combination, you could try scarlet-red cyclamen and dark green ivy. Although traditionally thought of as houseplants, these varieties will grow outdoors in a sheltered, frost-free position; the warmth given out from the walls of a house and shelter from an overhead porch may be sufficient in areas where the winter is relatively mild. When buying winter cherries, look for bushy plants with dark green leaves. There should be plenty of mostly still unripe, green berries; these will eventually turn orange and provide color until late winter.

6 Fill the gaps between plants with more soil and cover the surface with moss to prevent erosion when watering. Water well and allow to drain.

Solanum pseudocapsicum 'Thurino'

Cyclamen persicum

Hedera helix 'Hvid Kolibri'

Hedera helix 'Adam'

2 Line the front and sides of the basket with a thick layer of sphagnum moss as insulation and to prevent soil from seeping out. Add potting mix to fill the base of the basket to just below the level of moss shown in the photograph.

3 Break up pots of rooted ivy cuttings into manageable chunks ready for planting. Guide the trails of ivy carefully through the bars, resting the rootball on top of the soil. This arrangement uses four pots of ivy.

4 Pack in more moss around the neck of each clump of ivy and continue to build up the moss lining until it reaches the top of the basket. Plant two winter cherries towards the back, leaving a gap at the front.

5 Plant the cyclamen, tilting it slightly forward so that the handsome marbled foliage hangs over the edge of the basket. This also helps to prevent water from collecting in the crown, which could cause the cyclamen to rot.

Hanging baskets

These are the classic containers for dazzling displays and if you choose a succession of plants, you can enjoy color and interest the whole year through. This section has it all.

Contents

PLANTING UP A HANGING BASKET

Hanging baskets are the ideal way to decorate a doorway or a stretch of wall, and they can hang from the ends of pergola poles or on free-standing basket supports anywhere in the garden. They are traditionally used to create spectacular displays by blending together a mixture of upright, trailing and chunkier-shaped annual bedding plants in a wide range of colors. However, there are many variations. You could plant a large group of identical plants in the same basket to give the effect of a huge ball of blooms. You can design hanging gardens that complement nearby tubs by using similar plants or a matching color scheme. Another idea is to plant very long dangly and tough foliage houseplants with trailing annuals, such as lobelia, in baskets for the summer. And why not plant things that twine upwards? Black-eyed Susan, canary creeper and morning glories will drape themselves round the outside of a basket and cover the chains, brackets and nearby trellis with their huge colorful flowers.

1 Stand an open-weave wire basket on a bucket for stability and line it – this is green-dyed natural coconut fiber.

2 The lining should be thick enough to retain the soil. Fill the center of the basket with soilless potting mixture. Its light weight is ideal for baskets.

Dwarf pelargonium

6 Hang the basket in a spot where it will receive direct sun for at least half the day, but is sheltered from drying winds. Deadhead regularly.

French marigold

Trailing lobelia

Coleus

3 Assemble your plants; these include dwarf pelargonium, trailing lobelia and coleus. Plant the tallest flower in the middle of the basket; this will add height to the arrangement. As you plant, remove any yellow leaves or spent flowerheads.

4 One side of the basket will form the front of the display, so plant a pair of flowers, one on either side of the central plant, for a symmetrical arrangement.

5 Tuck in the coleus; choose plants with complementary colors. Coleus are grown for their foliage, so nip out the flower buds, otherwise leaves lose their color.

1 Place a flexible liner inside the basket. Press it well down and overlap adjacent panels to achieve a good fit.

USING A FLEXIBLE LINER

Many types of natural and synthetic flexible liners are available for use with traditional wire hanging baskets. These offer the best possible compromise between moss and a rigid liner. Flexible liners are made from a series of panels that, when pushed down inside the basket, overlap slightly to take up the shape of the container. They can be made of foam plastic, coconut fiber or the rather less flexible 'whalehide'. The advantage of this type of liner is that, where the panels overlap, you are left with small slits through which you can put the plants. This makes it possible to create the spectacular 'ball of bloom', characteristic of a traditional moss-lined basket. However, because the liner is made of a more water-retentive material, the basket will not dry out or drip as much as a mossed one. As with a traditional moss-lined basket, it is good idea to place an old saucer or circle of plastic into the base of the basket after lining, which helps to stop the water dripping straight out through the bottom.

6 Gather up the chains and hang up the basket. Water it well, allowing the potting mix to absorb some of the water before adding more, until it is moist through.

Ivy-leaved pelargonium 'Scarlet Galilee'

Single red petunia

Pink and red impatiens

Fuchsia 'Meike Meursing'

Helichrysum microphylla

2 Push the plant roots through the slits between the panels. Tuck the edges of the panels firmly around the plants to prevent soil from leaking out.

3 Fill the basket to the rim with potting mixture, making sure that it completely surrounds the roots of the plants that have already been put in.

4 Next, begin planting the top of the basket. These three bushy fuchsias will give some height among the other plants, which are predominantly trailing species.

5 Knock all the plants out of their pots first. Plant an ivy-leaved pelargonium (often called geranium) and petunias in the gaps between the fuchsias.

A SELF-WATERING HANGING BASKET

Hanging baskets dry out much faster than containers at ground level, so it is well worth considering a self-watering model. These have a built-in water reservoir in the base, into which a 'wick' dangles from the planting space above. To prime the system, simply fill the reservoir and water the potting mix, and capillary action will do the rest. Depending on the size of the plants and growing conditions, the reservoir should last two to five days between fills. There are a few other useful watering techniques that will help you. One is to mix water-retaining gel crystals into the soil before planting the basket. (They can be added after planting, if you stir them carefully into the potting mix between the plants, but it is not possible once the container is full of roots). Another technique is to sink a plastic soft drinks bottle, with the end cut off, into the middle of the basket where it is hidden by plants. Use this like a funnel to channel water right into the heart of the basket where it cannot run out over the sides when you water. You can leave the screw cap on the bottle and make a couple of pinholes in the neck so the water leaks out slowly and evenly during the day. (Add a few drops of liquid feed to the bottle, for 'little and often' feeding.)

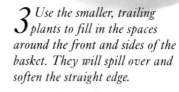

Pelargonium

Verbena

Argyranthemum

Petunia

4 Hang the basket in a sunny, but sheltered spot. Make sure that the 'best' side faces front. Top up the reservoir every two to three days as necessary.

1 Threequarters fill the basket with potting mix. Lightweight peat or coir are best in baskets. Avoid putting soil in the tube. Do not fill the water reservoir yet.

2 Place the taller plants between the attachment points for the chains, so that you get an uncluttered view when the basket is hanging up.

3 Use the smaller, trailing plants to fill in the spaces around the front and sides of the basket. They will spill over and soften the straight edge.

5 When the basket is full, water the plants in the usual way until the soil is evenly moist. Then fill the reservoir in the base by trickling water down the pipe in the center.

The capillary matting is in direct contact with the soil. If it is damp, so is the soil.

1 *Feed the wick through the plastic base plate. It draws water up from the reservoir at the base of the basket and keeps the capillary matting damp.*

2 *Push the watering tube through the hole in the base plate before adding any potting mixture and plants. You should be able to camouflage it easily.*

A SPRING BASKET

In this display, a fresh scheme of yellow and white spring flowers and foliage contrasts with a dark green, self-watering basket. As it has solid sides, pick at least one plant with long trails to soften the edge, such as the green-and-white variegated ivy used here. White drumstick primulas pick up on the white-edged ivy; their display is relatively long-lived, the spherical heads opening and developing over a number of weeks. When flowering has finished, transfer the plants to the garden, if possible to a spot with moisture-retentive soil and light shade. The glossy-leaved *Euonymus japonicus* 'Aureus' comes from the houseplant section of a garden center as little pots of rooted cuttings. When the basket is dismantled, you can separate these out and pot them up individually.

3 *Add a layer of moist potting mix, completely covering the capillary matting. Try the largest plant for size - here a primula - and adjust the level as necessary.*

4 *Gently tease the roots apart at the base, so that they spread out flat. Add another primula and fill in the gaps left on one side with the variegated* Euonymus.

6 *Hang the basket in a lightly shaded, sheltered spot, watering it via the tube. Cut off drumsticks when the whole head has finished flowering.*

Primula denticulata 'Alba'

Primula (hardy hybrid primrose)

Hedera helix *cultivar* (variegated ivy)

Euonymus japonicus 'Aureus'

5 *Plant two hardy primroses, one on either side of the watering tube. Split apart a couple of pots of rooted ivy cuttings and fit them around the edge. Fill any gaps with soil. Water the potting mixture thoroughly. As well as ivy, try variegated periwinkle, Aubretia or silver* Lamium.

A SMALL HANGING BASKET

Hanging basket schemes need not be large, extravagant and multicolored. Those planned around a single color can be very effective, too. The secret is to make maximum use of contrasting shapes and textures. Seek out plants whose flowers are the same color, but different in shape and size. Where possible, choose plants with silvery gray or felty leaves as a change from plain green. Look for foliage with different sizes and textures, too. Use some large, leathery leaves and some small, airy leaves like those of ferns. And even if you are planning a single color for your theme, do try to bring in touches of a second color, even if it is not particularly noticeable, as this gives the whole arrangement depth. A good way to create a color scheme is to introduce a totally contrasting color, but in very small amounts. Many flowers have a different colored 'eye' in the center and this would be a good second color to use for a natural highlight.

4 The trailing plant should scramble around the other two without smothering them. Plant them against the back. They should be a little taller than the trailer, but not over-dominant.

Petunia

5 Hang the arrangement in a sheltered, sunny spot, so that the trailing plant faces front. In this model, the chains can be detached from the hook for ease of planting.

Cockscomb (Celosia cristata)

Scaevola aemula

1 Rest the basket on top of a bucket while you plant it up. Put in the liner and fill it with potting mix. Peat-based types hold moisture best.

2 Plant trailing or sprawling plants at the front of the basket. Turn the plant round so that it naturally leans over the edge and soon makes a good display.

3 The other plants in this display pick out the two colors, blue and yellow, in the flowers of the large sprawling plant that forms the centerpiece.

A CLASSIC HANGING BASKET

The best time to plant a hanging basket is early summer, after the frosts. However, if you have a frost-free greenhouse or sunroom, you can plant it in late spring and keep it under cover until the weather is warm enough to put it outside. ('Harden' the plants off first by putting the basket out on fine days and then bringing it in at night for the first week or two.) Wire hanging baskets are traditionally lined with sphagnum moss. Soak it first so that it is easier to work with and place it green side down in the base of the basket. Summer bedding are the most popular plants for hanging baskets. Traditional favorites include trailing plants, such as petunias, ivy-leaved pelargoniums, fuchsia teamed with lobelia, and compact, upright plants, such as *Impatiens*, French marigolds, tuberous begonias and zonal pelargoniums. These plants will flower throughout the summer.

4 Plant the top of the basket from the center outwards to avoid damaging the plants. Turn the basket round as you work. Put the tallest plants in the center for best effect.

5 The petunia is sprawling out around the edges. Put the remaining plants in rootball-to-rootball to pack in as many as possible for instant impact.

6 With a traditional spherical planting scheme like this the basket will completely disappear beneath a glorious mass of flowers.

Pelargonium 'Coco Rico'

Fuchsia

Impatiens

Petunia 'Express Red Star'

Lobelia 'Blue Fountain'

1 Place thick wads of moss in the base of the basket. Tuck trailing lobelia through the edge of the base, resting the roots on the moss. Space the plants evenly.

2 Now tuck a few larger plants through the basket sides. Push the roots through from outside so they reach well into the center and rest on the ledge of moss.

3 Complete the mossing of the sides, taking the moss slightly above the rim of the basket to retain the soil. Fill with a peat-based potting mixture.

A HERB HANGING BASKET

A hanging basket is a useful way to grow culinary varieties of herbs, as you can put it right outside the kitchen door, where it acts as a herbal air freshener, giving the house a pleasant, healthy perfume each time you open the door and brush past the plants. The scent of herbs is also said to deter flies. Choose popular culinary varieties that are naturally compact, such as bush basil. As the basket will be replanted every spring, you have the chance to replace annual herbs, such as basil and chervil, and also to divide up over-large clumps of perennials, such as mint and chives. Rosemary roots easily from cuttings and parsley is a biennial that runs to seed in its second year, so replace it each spring with new seedlings. As well as taller plants for the center of the basket, you will need a few trailing ones, such as thyme and marjoram, to plant around the sides, and try to include some with colored leaves or bright flowers. Pick them regularly to keep them neat and bushy and feed and water them well.

1 Remove the detachable 'pockets' and plant into them from inside or outside, whichever is easier.

3 Plant the larger herbs in the top of the basket. Some varieties of mint can 'take over', but this pineapple mint is a less vigorous one.

2 If the plant has a large rootball, plant it from the inside, pushing the top of the plant through the side hole. Almost fill the pot with potting mix.

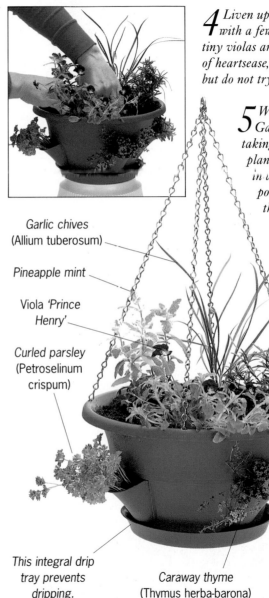

4 Liven up a herb collection with a few flowers. These tiny violas are a close relative of heartsease, a medicinal herb, but do not try to eat them.

5 Water the basket well. Gather up the chains, taking care not to snag the plants. Hang the basket in a sunny but sheltered position, ideally close to the kitchen door.

Garlic chives (Allium tuberosum)

Pineapple mint

Viola 'Prince Henry'

Curled parsley (Petroselinum crispum)

Rosemary (Rosmarinus officinalis)

This integral drip tray prevents dripping.

Caraway thyme (Thymus herba-barona)

Dwarf marjoram (Origanum vulgare 'Compactum')

PLANTING A BASKET OF FUCHSIAS

Most people would agree that the ideal way to view fuchsia flowers is when they are growing in a hanging basket. You can really see them in all their glory from below or, best of all, at eye level. For the best effect, restrict each basket to only one variety of fuchsia; if you mix them, they begin to look messy, as different varieties will grow at different rates and flower at different times. The number of plants that you put in a basket depends on the size of the basket. Always plant one in the middle, otherwise you can end up with a hole as the plants begin to grow downwards. The plants will need regular pinching out after every two or three pairs of leaves to achieve a longer, but not straggly, look. To ensure that the basket flowers continuously for many months, remove dead flowerheads and seedpods and feed it regularly. Use a slow-release fertilizer if the basket is difficult to reach for liquid feeding. Turn the basket regularly to make sure that it retains a balanced shape.

5 This basket of Ballet Girl is coming into flower 10–12 weeks after the final stop. The blooms are hanging over the sides of the basket and will soon cascade in all directions.

1 Choose a peat-based potting mix, which is lighter for a hanging basket. Select a suitable cultivar; an odd number of plants creates the best effect.

2 Place a little potting mix in the base of the basket and then position all the plants except one around the edge of the container in a symmetrical pattern.

Pinching out, or stopping, the plants encourages bushy growth and controls their shape.

3 Finally add the central plant. This one will prevent a hole appearing at the top of the basket once the plants start to grow. Fill the gaps between the plants with soil, but do not push it down.

4 Fix the chains onto the basket, so that the plants can grow around them without being damaged. Tie the chains securely to a cane to keep them well above the growing plants.

HOSTAS FOR A SHADY PLACE

With the exception of the variegated ivy, all the plants in this basket come from the herbaceous perennials section of the garden center. There is no reason why plants from any category - alpine, shrub, herbaceous or houseplant - cannot be used temporarily in a hanging basket, providing they are the right size with an attractive habit and long-lasting color, but the more drought-tolerant types are obviously better suited. A number of flowering bedding plants thrive in shade, including *Fuchsia*, *Impatiens*, *Lobelia* and *Begonia*. Team them with ivies or gold-leaved foliage plants, such as the feathery golden feverfew (*Tanacetum parthenium* 'Aureum'), golden creeping Jenny (*Lysimachia nummularia* 'Aurea') or a gold-leaved hosta. Silver and gray-leaved plants do not normally tolerate shade, which is why the silver-leaved lamiums, including 'White Nancy' and 'Pink Pewter', make such useful basket plants. Some of the fernlike dicentras associated with woodland gardening also work well in shade. Here, 'Pearl Drops' makes a wonderful contrast with the golden hosta.

1 Many liners are made from recycled or waste materials; this coir matting is a by-product of the coconut industry. Wool, foam and paper are also used.

2 Pour in some moisture-retentive potting mixture - one designed for hanging baskets is ideal. Here, the thick liner also helps to protect the plants from drying out.

3 Plant the dicentra - this is 'Pearl Drops' - and then add the gold-leaved hosta 'August Moon'. As well as strikingly architectural foliage, it produces pale pink bellflower spikes in midsummer.

Dicentra 'Pearl Drops' has blue-gray foliage.

Hosta 'August Moon'

5 Hang the basket in a sheltered shady site. At the end of the season, you could transfer the plants to a wooden half barrel with dwarf spring bulbs.

Gold-variegated Hedera helix cultivar (ivy)

Lamium maculatum 'Pink Pewter'

4 Add the lamium and ivy. Fill in any gaps with potting mix. Add a thick layer of moist sphagnum moss or fine chipped bark as a water-retaining mulch.

A WINTER HANGING BASKET

Given a reasonably sheltered sunny spot, it is possible to keep hanging baskets looking good all winter. Choose from the limited range of suitable flowers backed up by plenty of evergreens. The most reliable winter flowers are 'universal' pansies and hybrid primroses. Add small evergreens such as ivy, euonymus, santolina or periwinkle (variegated versions are especially pretty). Use the trailing kinds around the edge for a fuller, softer effect. In big cities, the microclimate often makes it possible to grow relatively tender plants outdoors in winter; almost hardy indoor plants such as cyclamen, winter cherry, cineraria and asparagus fern often thrive. You can reuse summer hanging baskets for winter displays, but avoid those with built-in drip trays or water reservoirs unless the basket is to be kept under cover – excess watering can be a problem in winter.

1 Threequarters fill the basket with potting mix. This leaves room for the rootballs of your plants, which will fill the top 3 inches of space in the basket.

Remove plants from their pots before planting.

2 Put in the plants without disturbing the rootballs. (This ensures that the flowers and buds do not receive a check in growth that could abort them.) Tuck them close together.

3 Add trailing ivies around the edges; they will partly cover the sides of the basket and create a fuller, more rounded display.

4 When all the plants are in, trickle some potting mixture between the rootballs so that no roots are left exposed to the air, then water thoroughly. Add more soil if some has been washed down into the basket.

5 Hang the basket in a sunny sheltered spot – a porch or under a car port is ideal – otherwise on a wall that receives the sun. Check to see if it needs watering every week, and apply a weak liquid feed when the weather is mild.

Plants in hanging baskets must be able to withstand exposure to severe weather.

Winter-flowering pansies

Cultivated primrose hybrids (Primula acaulis hybrids)

Variegated ivy

RESCUING A DRIED-OUT HANGING BASKET

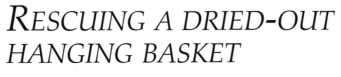

Containers need attention little and often to keep them looking their best. The important thing to remember is that they need more water as the plants in them grow bigger. Large plants use more water and feed than when they were small, and once their roots fill the soil, there is less room for water. As long as the plants are not completely dead, a container can usually be revived. The first aim is to get some water into the soil. Unless you used water-retaining gel crystals in the soil before planting, dried out potting mix is very difficult to rewet, so try adding a tiny drop of liquid detergent to the water as a wetting agent. The simplest solution is to stand the container in a deep bowl of water for at least an hour until the soil is completely saturated. Here we show how to rescue and tidy up a typical 'lost cause.'

1 This moss-lined basket has been rather neglected; the soil is bone dry, the moss is yellow and the flowers need deadheading, trimming and tying up into place.

5 Tie back healthy green shoots with plenty of flower, using loose twist ties or thin string. Trailing and climbing plants look best growing up the chains or trained round the sides.

6 Stand the basket in a deep bowl of tepid water for at least an hour and spray the plants to revive them. This also helps the potting mix to start absorbing water.

2 Start by snipping off the dead flowerheads - this makes the basket look better straightaway. Remove any dead, damaged or browning leaves at the same time.

3 Where there are no buds on the same shoot to follow on, cut complete stems back close to the base to encourage a new crop of shoots and buds.

4 Tease trailing stems apart and see which pieces are worth keeping. Cut old, yellowing shoots with no new buds back to where they branch from a healthy shoot.

A small hand sprayer is ideal for misting the plants.

REGENERATING A LOPSIDED HANGING BASKET

If they are close to a wall, where they receive light from one side while the other is in heavy shade, container plants sometimes grow lopsided. The answer is to turn the containers round every week or two, so that both sides have a turn in the light. However, because of their shape, some plants naturally grow to one side more than the other, so choose well-shaped bushy specimens in the first place. (If you raise plants from seed or cuttings, nip the growing tips out when they are 2–3 inches high.) Prevent plants growing lopsided by checking them over regularly, nip out any shoots that are growing out of place and cut straggly or one-sided growth back quite hard. This encourages the plant to branch out from lower down, producing several shoots where there was previously one.

1 This basket has been growing close to a wall, with one side in shade. Because it has not been turned regularly, the plants have all grown over to one side.

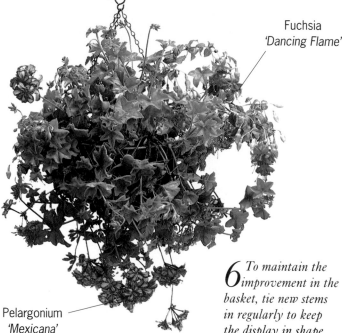

Fuchsia 'Dancing Flame'

Pelargonium 'Mexicana'

6 To maintain the improvement in the basket, tie new stems in regularly to keep the display in shape.

2 With the basket still hanging up, have a quick tidy up and snip off all the dead flowerheads. With fuchsias, take off the heads at the point where the flower stems join the main plant stem.

3 Lift the basket down and stand it in the top of a bucket. Remove any dead leaves and flowers, spread out the stems and space them out around the basket. Tie them around the rim with plant ties.

If you need more height, stand the bucket on an upturned bowl.

4 Carefully separate long trailing stems that have become tangled together and spread them out as much as possible all round the basket to give it a more even coverage.

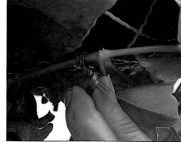

5 When the basket is hanging back up on its bracket, tie these stems in place evenly over the underside of the basket – this creates a much more impressive-looking sphere of flowers.

Vegetables and herbs

Even if you do not normally grow your own vegetables and herbs, try some of the ideas in this section and you will be pleasantly surprised at how easy and fulfilling it can be.

Contents

1 *Never try to pull a plant from its pot; turn it upside-down, tap the rim on a bench and let the plant drop gently into your hand. This rootball is full of healthy, strong roots.*

2 *Scoop out a planting hole in the growing bag. This usually means going right down to the bottom of the bag to get it deep enough.*

TOMATOES IN A GROWING BAG

One of the best ways of growing tomatoes, in a greenhouse and outdoors, is in a growing bag. Tomatoes are susceptible to root diseases at the best of times and greenhouse plants are especially vulnerable. Growing bags are free of pests and diseases and the plastic isolates plant roots from any diseased soil. Both single stem (disbudded) and bush varieties grow well in bags. Generally speaking, grow one less plant of a bush variety than a disbudded one, because a bush type takes up more room. Follow the general rules for watering growing bags; wait until the surface of the soil has dried out and then give at least a gallon of water at a time. Feeding is not necessary for the first few weeks, but once the first fruits are pea-sized, feed according to the instructions on the bag or the bottle. To allow sun and air to reach the bottom fruits, remove the leaves from the base of the plant up to the lowest truss that has fruit showing red. Tomatoes dislike high growing temperatures, so make sure that the greenhouse is adequately ventilated and shaded. Too much heat leads to excessive water loss and this can cause problems, notably blossom end rot, which causes affected tomatoes to turn black at the base.

3 *Firm the plant gently but adequately into place. Never be tempted to push the soil down too hard or you run the risk of it becoming waterlogged.*

4 *Put in three plants per bag in a greenhouse. Outdoors, plant four single stem, but only three bush plants per bag.*

TOMATOES IN A GROWING BAG

5 *Give the soil a good soaking by applying up to 1.5 gallons of water at the first watering. Later waterings can be slightly less.*

6 *The same growing bag some weeks later. Being a bush variety, the side shoots have not been removed from the plant, so flowers abound with the promise of a good crop.*

Below right: The tomatoes on this bush variety are maturing, providing an attractive array of colors from pale green to bright red. Single stem varieties in growing bags in a greenhouse should grow to six or seven fruit trusses high; outdoors expect to ripen four or five trusses. In both cases, nip out the plant at two leaves above the top truss.

When to plant out tomatoes

The tomato on the left is too young to plant out. Extra growth induced by putting it into new soil will lead to an unfruitful bottom truss. The tomato at right has the first flower open and is ready to plant out. Buy suitable plants from garden centers.

119

1 Fill the container almost full with a good multipurpose potting mixture. Firm it down gently at this stage to prevent compaction later on.

BROAD BEANS IN A TUB

Broad beans are very easy to cultivate and make splendid plants for growing in containers on a sunny patio if you do not have room in the garden. The dwarf varieties are short and sturdy and generally need no support; choose 'The Sutton' for this type of gardening. Never grow broad beans under cover once they are more than about 4 inches tall; any extra warmth will draw them up and they soon become leggy and topple over. Make sure you keep them outdoors, so that the flowers are adequately pollinated by bees. Because the dwarf varieties are not hardy enough to withstand the winter outdoors, sow them in the early spring. Unfortunately, this means that they are as susceptible to attacks of blackfly in the summer as are all the other spring varieties (Longpod and Windsor types), but luckily, this pest is easy to control. Besides removing the tip of each shoot once young beans are forming, spray any affected plants with a suitable chemical that will destroy aphids. Any systemic insecticide will do this, but a spray containing just pirimicarb is more acceptable as it only kills the aphids.

5 Now you can see the benefits of growing only dwarf varieties. The plants stay short and are much better suited to growing in containers.

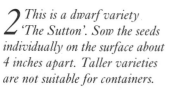

2 This is a dwarf variety 'The Sutton'. Sow the seeds individually on the surface about 4 inches apart. Taller varieties are not suitable for containers.

3 Push the seeds into the potting mixture with your finger so that they end up 1.5-2 inches deep. Move some soil back over the seeds and firm in gently.

4 Water the container thoroughly. Carry out the initial watering in easy stages but do not stop until you see some water draining out of the base.

6 The young plants are growing well and in flower. When grown outdoors, where it is cooler, this variety needs no support.

1 Buy seed potatoes in early spring and sit them on end to sprout. Keep them in cool to normal room conditions in daylight.

POTATOES IN A TUB

You can grow all kinds of potatoes in containers, but it is more practical to grow early (new) potatoes or 'specialist' varieties that are difficult to find in the shops. The crop should be ready by early to midsummer, leaving the container free to be planted up with flowers or other edibles, such as herbs. Early potatoes are ready to pick when the first flowers appear on the plants. There is no need to pull up the whole plant; just feel round for the largest potatoes and leave the others to grow for a bit longer. Leave maincrop potatoes until the foliage starts to yellow naturally before pulling them up, but again you can take a few potatoes before this stage. Keep potatoes well fed and watered during the growing period and buy new seed potatoes the following year.

5 Space another three potatoes into the gaps between the potatoes in the previous layer. This way, the tub will be virtually full.

6 Fill the tub with soil to within 1 inch of the rim. Put it in a sunny sheltered spot. Thoroughly moisten the soil, but do not overwater.

7 When the plants are growing strongly, keep them regularly watered and feed them every ten days with any good-quality, general-purpose liquid feed.

2 Shovel 3 inches of potting mixture into the bottom of a large container. You could reuse old growing bag soil, as long as it has not been used for growing potatoes before.

3 When the sprouts on the seed potatoes are ½–1 inch long, lay them on the soil in the tub, about 10 inches apart, with the sprouts facing upwards. This tub is big enough to take three.

4 Shovel another 2 inches of potting mixture into the tub, just deep enough to bury the first lot of potatoes. To achieve maximum productivity, you could fit in a second 'tier' of potatoes.

GROWING ZUCCHINI

Zucchini will thrive in a sunny position in fertile soil well supplied with bulky organic matter. Like pumpkins, squashes and cucumbers, they are half-hardy and even the slightest touch of frost can kill them. This means that in a cool temperate climate you must sow them and grow on the seedlings in a greenhouse or a sunny room until they are large enough to plant outside after the risk of frost is over. Sow seeds under cover in mid-spring. Alternatively, plant them outdoors in late spring where they are to grow. Once they start fruiting, pick over the plants regularly and often to ensure a good succession of zucchini. Try not to let them reach more than about 6 inches long. The best varieties of zucchini are those with a bushy habit; they take up much less room than the trailing type and are perfect for most gardens.

4 A good initial watering is vital for these plants. It also helps prevent red spider mites becoming established; they dislike a damp atmosphere.

Some particularly prolific varieties will continue fruiting over a long period.

5 A few weeks later, the plants are growing nicely. Ignore the slight difference in foliage; this is a varietal characteristic and not harmful.

1 Raise zucchini in individual peat pots. Water well and put them in a plastic bag in a warm place to germinate. When they come through, put in full light.

2 Given warmth, young plants grow quickly and are ready for potting on or planting out when a good number of roots appear through the sides of the peat pot.

3 Leave the top of the rootball ½ inch above the soil. This part of the plant is vulnerable to collar rot fungus disease, and leaving it exposed like this means that it is able to dry out.

Put two plants in a standard-size growing bag.

6 With the right care and plenty of water, you can have zucchini all summer. Always grow a proper zucchini variety; a vegetable marrow will not do.

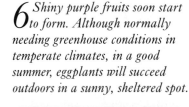

1 Sow eggplant seeds singly in small pots and plant them out into a growing bag in a greenhouse or sunroom when they have made a good root system. Three plants in a standard-sized growing bag is ample, as they will grow to make large plants.

GROWING EGGPLANTS

To raise eggplants successfully, it is important that they have sufficient heat. It is better to leave the sowing until early to mid-spring or be prepared to keep them warm. Do not overdo the heat, though, or they will become drawn, weak and useless. Aim at a temperature around 60°F. Never be tempted to take too many fruits from a plant or the size will suffer; four is ample. In a greenhouse, eggplants are especially susceptible to attacks of red spider mite. Although the plants are fairly well able to stand up for themselves, the mite will spread to other species, with disastrous results.

There is no reliable chemical control for red spider mite, but the predatory mite *Phytoseiulus* produces excellent results if you introduce it as soon as the leaves start to show signs of speckling in the summer.

6 Shiny purple fruits soon start to form. Although normally needing greenhouse conditions in temperate climates, in a good summer, eggplants will succeed outdoors in a sunny, sheltered spot.

2 The top of the rootball should be just below the soil level. Firming in the plants excludes air pockets and ensures that water is readily absorbed by the roots.

3 Water thoroughly with at least a gallon of water. This should be all that is needed for 10–14 days. Do not feed the plants at this stage.

4 When the stem is 6–8 inches tall, nip out the top to encourage a good number of side shoots to form. This also prevents the plant from getting too tall.

5 On these plants the side shoots are growing vigorously and the first flowers are beginning to show.

1 Fill the pot with potting mixture until you nearly reach the level of the planting spaces – in taller pots, these might appear at various heights.

PLANTING UP A POT OF FRESH PARSLEY

Parsley is one of the most used herbs in the kitchen, but it does not dry well, so it is worth growing it yourself to ensure a fresh supply. If space is limited, the answer might be multipocketed strawberry barrels, which suit parsley just as well and are perfect for backyards and patios. A partly shady spot is ideal for parsley and be sure to provide plenty of moisture. Parsley is a biennial and the leaves taste best in the first year, becoming bitter and rather coarse in the second, so try to sow a fresh supply each year in spring and late summer. The seeds can take at least six weeks to germinate, but this can be speeded up by soaking them overnight in warm water and then soaking a fine tilth seed bed with boiling water before planting. Cover the seeds thinly with fine soil and thin the seedlings to about 10 inches apart. For a fresh supply of parsley all winter, sow seeds in the greenhouse in midsummer or pot up the roots of spring-grown plants to bring indoors.

2 Once you have released each plant by upturning and tapping the pot, you may need to squeeze the rootball slightly to make it fit through the holes. Avoid damaging the roots.

3 Insert the parsley plants into the planting holes, pressing them firmly into the potting mixture. Make sure that the rootball is covered and the plants are the right way up.

4 Place the final plant in the top of the container, making sure that it is planted at the correct height so that it grows right out of the top.

5 After filling and firming with potting mixture, sprinkle a handful of small stones or gravel over the surface. This helps to reduce moisture loss.

Curled parsley (Petroselinum crispum) *has dense foliage.*

6 The finished pot provides plenty of parsley for picking within a very small planted area. Pinch off flower stalks as they appear to maintain good growth.

PLANTING A BAY TREE

Most people think of bay as a shrubby evergreen bush or decorative standard tree. The leaves are the main attraction, being large, shiny, deep green and highly aromatic. They can be picked and used at any time, but dry well too, the flavor actually strengthening and becoming more mellow. Native to the Mediterranean, this handsome laurel is susceptible to frosts, so may need protection even in warm climates. In cooler ones, plant the bay in a tub for overwintering in the greenhouse or conservatory. It does not grow well from seed so is usually propagated from cuttings, best taken in early summer. Bay prefers a light, well-drained soil, but grows slowly even in sunny, sheltered conditions. This makes it expensive to buy as a mature plant, but an excellent herb for trimming and clipping into formal shapes.

4 When the plant is in place, continue filling the pot with more of the soil, taking care that the bay remains upright and in the correct position. Try to avoid getting any soil on the foliage.

Make sure that the bay is planted at the same depth as it was in its original container.

A layer of small stones or gravel on the surface of the soil not only helps to retain moisture, but also looks attractive and discourages weed growth.

1 Good drainage is essential if the bay tree is to grow successfully, so add a few crocks in the bottom of the pot – it is worth saving any pieces of broken plant pot for this purpose.

2 Start filling the container with a light, sterilized soil. Synthetic particles are available to improve drainage. Make sure that the pot you use has been scrubbed and sterilized, too.

3 Take the bay out of its pot and lower it gently into the new container, holding the stem gently between your fingers and supporting the foliage against your hand.

5 Stand the bay in a sunny, sheltered spot and bring it under cover at the first sign of frost. It produces small yellow-green flowers in late spring or early summer, followed by black berries.

SHAPING A BAY TREE

1 *A newly planted bay tree will need light trimming to provide the first outline of its future shape. Carefully insert a firm, upright stake in the center of the pot.*

2 *Secure the main stem of the bay tree to the stake using string or a wire clip as shown here. Do not tighten too much – allow space for the stem to grow.*

Once planted, the bay tree *(Laurus nobilis)* is easy to care for and can attain a mature height of 13-15 feet. Water it every day during the growing season, especially in hot weather. In winter, when the plant has been brought inside and growth is slow, it will only require watering if the soil feels really dry. If the bay is growing in a container, feed it every week with a nitrogen feed from spring until the end of the summer to encourage healthy new leaves. Bay trees in pots can look particularly attractive when trained and shaped to grow into pyramids, balls and other topiary shapes. It is a useful way of removing leaves required for the kitchen and you can dry surplus leaves for later use. The leaves of green bay may be smooth or crinkly at the edges. Other forms of bay include *L. n.* 'Aurea', with bright gold leaves in spring and *L. n.* 'Angustifolia', the willow leaf bay.

3 *Having decided on a shape, trim the long shoots to neaten the general appearance. This bay is too small to start removing branches from the main stem to form a standard.*

Repot into a larger container after about a year or when the roots are visibly filling the soil.

4 *As this is the first trim on a young bay, leave the sides and base wider than the top. If you remove too many leaves at one time, it may slow down growth.*

5 *Leave the stake in place until the main stem is firm enough to remain erect. If you remove uneven growth as it appears, the rounded shape will develop as the bush grows and slowly expands. Examine the shape from all sides.*

The leaves add a deep, lasting fragrance to potpourri, as well as being ideal for cooking.

CREATING A HERB GARDEN FOR A WINDOW LEDGE

A windowbox is the perfect way to grow a selection of culinary herbs in the minimum of space. The kitchen window ledge is an obvious site, providing the window opens conveniently enough for regular access to your mini garden. Make absolutely sure that the windowbox is firmly secured; use strong brackets or ties and check these periodically for wear or weathering. The box might be home-made from new or old planks of wood, painted to match window frames or shutters; or it might be lightweight plastic, antique stone or terracotta. If you feel that the windows are too exposed a site, why not plant up an indoor windowbox, which will make a perfect home for a few of the more tender species, such as basil.

2 Take out the plants and arrange a few crocks or broken pieces of pot in the bottom to prevent the potting mixture washing away.

1 Choose a selection of herbs, preferably with a variety of foliage shapes and textures. Stand them in the box to see how they look together.

Herbs in the kitchen

The flavor of fresh herbs is far more delicate than that of dried ones, so use them generously. Generally speaking, add them at the end of cooking for maximum effect. Mint, basil and tarragon change their flavor once dried. Add fresh, chopped herbs to soups and salads; tie them in tiny bundles to add to stocks and stews; or tuck sprigs of rosemary, sage or thyme under a roast joint to bring out the flavor.

3 Herbs need good drainage, so add 2-6 inches of washed gravel or pea shingle for a well-draining layer at the bottom of the box. Top up with planting mixture.

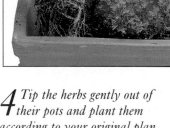

4 Tip the herbs gently out of their pots and plant them according to your original plan. Try to maintain a balance of appearance, height and habit.

CREATING A HERB GARDEN FOR A WINDOW LEDGE

Regular cropping or trimming is important to ensure that herbs remain small and leafy. Keep the box adequately watered and apply a liquid feed during the growing and cropping season. The soil soon runs out of essential nutrients in the confines of a box. A mulch of small pebbles conserves moisture and reduces the effect of heavy rains.

6 *A sprinkling of gravel or decorative small stones on top of the soil around the plants looks attractive and helps to slow down moisture loss.*

7 *The finished trough looks good and includes a useful blend of flavors for the cook. If you use plenty of herbs in cooking, reduce the number of plants in the box to two or three bigger plants.*

5 *Top up with soil, making sure it settles between the plants without any air gaps. Remember to leave a space at the top for watering.*

Chives
(Allium schoenoprasum)

Sage
(Salvia officinalis)

Culinary thyme
(Thymus vulgaris)

Parsley
(Petroselinum crispum)

French tarragon
(Artemisia dracunculus)

Sorrel (Rumex acetosa)

Oregano
(Origanum vulgare)